# witness specialist moderator

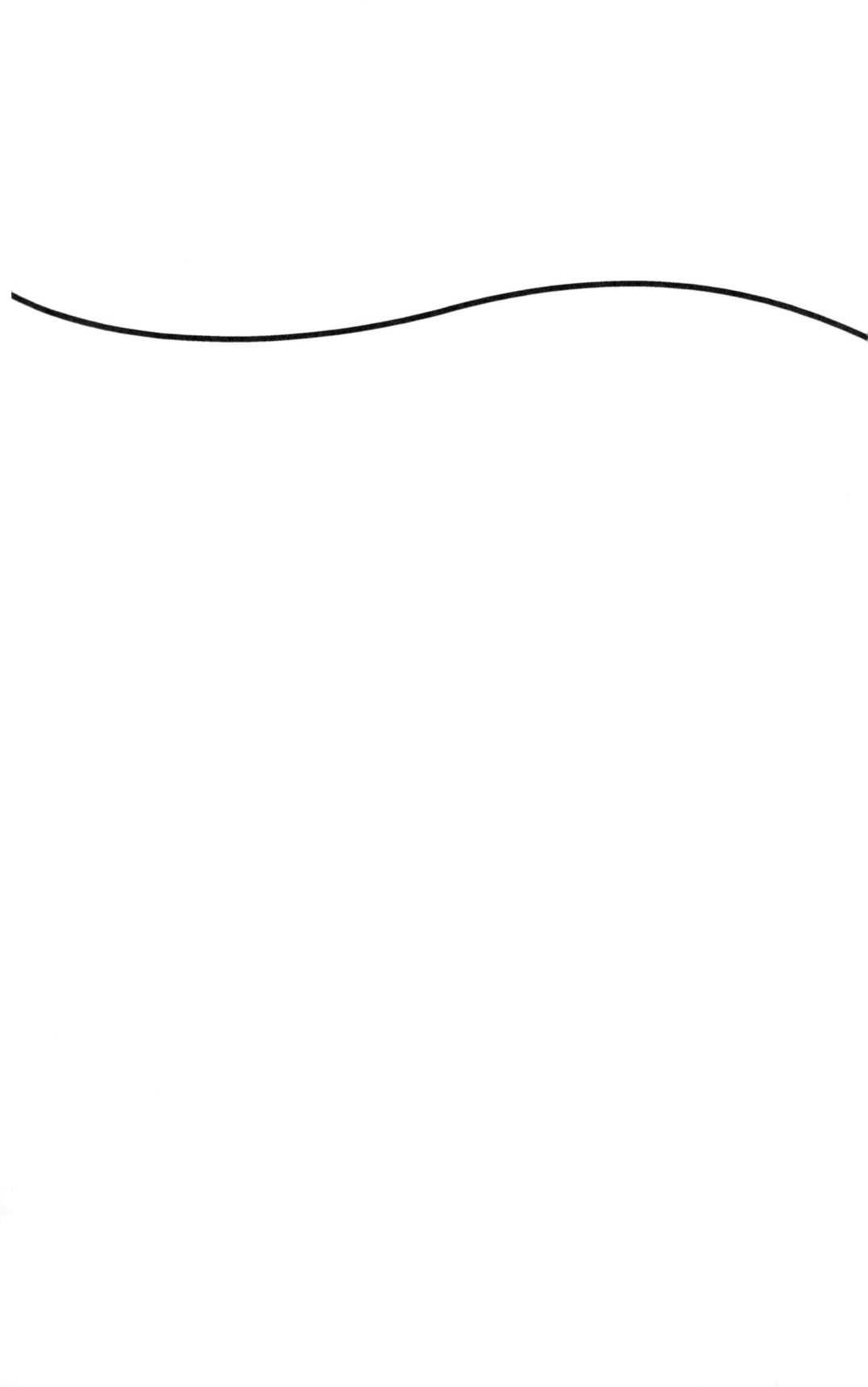

# witness
# specialist
# moderator

the critical role of
Catholic Educators in
our changing world

**Bernadette Mercieca & Ann Rennie**

Published in Australia by
Garratt Publishing
32 Glenvale Crescent
Mulgrave, VIC 3170
www.garrattpublishing.com.au

Copyright in this work remains the property of the contributing authors.

Copyright © 2023 Bernadette Mercieca & Ann Rennie

All rights reserved. Except as provided by the Australian copyright law, no part of this book may be reproduced in any way without permission in writing from the publisher.

Cover by Guy Holt
Cover image and page 182 © iStock
Inside images supplied by authors
Typesetting by Mike Kuszla
Edited by Greg Hill

Scripture quotations are drawn from the New Revised Standard Version of the Bible, copyright © 1989 by the Division of Christian Education of the National Council of the Churches of Christ in the USA.
Used by permission.
All rights reserved.

ISBN 9781922484741

A catalogue record for this book is available from the National Library of Australia

Cataloguing in Publication information for this title is available from the National Library of Australia.
www.nla.gov.au

The authors and publisher gratefully acknowledge the permission granted to reproduce the copyright material in this book. Every effort has been made to trace copyright holders and to obtain their permission for the use of copyright material.

The publisher apologises for any errors or omissions in the above list and would be grateful if notified of any corrections that should be incorporated in future reprints or editions of this book.

*We dedicate this book in gratitude to our first educators in faith:
our parents, Margaret and Des Harty and James and Barbara O'Neill.*

*For their understanding that the writing of this book was a priority for us, we also dedicate this book with love to our husbands,
Paul and Robert.*

*We offer our thanks for those many teachers who encouraged us
as we grew up.*

*We honour the memory of those pioneering religious congregations who founded schools across the country. In particular, The Faithful Companions of Jesus and The Institute Of the Blessed Virgin Mary (IBVM) – Loreto Sisters.*

*We continue in solidarity and companionship with all those who teach in Catholic schools today, in the hope of the ongoing mission of Catholic education in Australia.*

***Bernadette & Ann***

*Bernadette and Ann have lived this book for decades. Every idea has been tested in the rough and tumble of the classroom. Don't look here for high falutin theories. Come to appreciate the passion and resilience of women who actually know what spiritual formation is all about. Somewhere along the way, we have forgotten that religious education is not just a sacred trust but also a truckload of fun. Bernadette and Ann remind us with wisdom and grace.*

– Michael McGirr
Author, Mission Director of Caritas Australia

*In this book, Bernadette and Ann lead us in a journey through their lives. Personal and humble, the touching text is accompanied by emotive images that together weave a story of two Australian women showing the importance of the Person in the Professional. Beginning with their own formative years, we progress through the book to acquire a keen insight to the current context of Catholic Religious Education in Australia. Not only does it provide the reader with concrete examples of present-day approaches and theories on RE in Australia, it can easily transfer to other educational settings, prompting deep reflection and meaningful discourse for religious educators the world over. It is an important contribution to document these personal memoirs of two witnesses, specialists and moderators and overall leaves the reader with a strong sense of hope for Catholic Religious Education in the future.*

– Dr Bernadette Sweetman
Post-doctoral researcher, Dublin City University

# Preface

This book has arisen out of a friendship that has grown between two Religious Education (RE) teachers, who have spent almost their entire professional careers involved in Catholic education in Victoria. Both of us were raised in strong Catholic families in the 1960s, one in Melbourne, the other in regional Victoria. In the course of our respective working lives we came to know each other, and eighteen months ago it transpired that we had a similar strong feeling about the state of Religious Education in Australian Catholic schools. As we look towards the end of our professional lives, we want to do what we can to pass on what we know to the next generation of teachers, especially those who will take up the gift and challenge of this faith-based discipline.

We feel that Religious Education is battling a crisis, the same crisis the Church is confronted with in this secular age. It is the crisis of relevance that is impacting many former institutional strongholds that are now looking outdated. Care and attention needs to be taken as we go forward with this, the educational mission of the Church.

Younger teachers may view this book as a primer to help them in discerning their own faith story. It may assist them in how they might travel differently with new understanding, enthusiasm, and commitment. Pre-service teachers will also find it helps to provide background details about Vatican II and the story of how Religious Education has changed in recent decades.

This book is our best effort in sharing our knowledge and experience, what got us to where we are now as we move towards the end of our professional careers and pass the baton on. We hope that it will illuminate your own teaching journey as you offer your own best effort to those you will educate.

~

We experienced the final days of a pre-Vatican II Church and the earliest euphoria of a Church grappling with the challenges of Vatican II. We have seen the Church grow and change over many decades, alongside parallel developments in school RE programs aiming to catechise and evangelise. We have grown older and (perhaps) wiser as the world has become more secular and pluralist and has raised issues of faith affiliation and the state of the worshipping community.

We hope that this book, and the questions we have provided at the end of each chapter, will guide reflection by individuals and groups. It is hoped that as the reader processes each section, it will give them pause to consider the implications of their own *witness, specialist, moderator* experiences to see where they stand in the light of their own Catholic identity and the consequent desire to share this with the rich diversity of children in our schools. We understand that the reader's formative experiences may well be very different to ours, but that difference also offers an entry point into the reality of the world today and a recognition that new approaches need to be taken for these changing and challenging, some would say liminal, times in Catholic education.

In this book we have offered thoughts and advice from our long involvement and experience in the teaching of Religious Education. We also understand that some of the language, ideas and images of the recent past may appear unfamiliar to future generations. Thus nuanced and sensitive treatment is needed in the contemporary classroom, so that the richness of the tradition is upheld whilst navigating the currents of the time.

## Preface

We hope that we have provided context for the Religious Education landscape in our Catholic schools and that it will be useful for those teachers who are taking up the challenge of helping students make meaning of their life in the culture in which they are immersed. It may also be a reminder of the recent past in Australia and where we find ourselves now as a consequence of vast and irrevocable social change. Our broad personal sweep over the previous half century may resonate with experiences and understandings that have been passed on in family, school and parish circumstances. In this book we trust that there have been moments of recognition, as well as moments of departure, as the as readers look back own formative and professional growth to see how and where it has led them to where they are today.

As we emphasise in the later chapters, Catholic schools and higher education institutions need to actively support graduating students to study theological and religious educational subjects as part of their degree. Perhaps this may lead to a commitment to returning to the Catholic system to teach. This is a significant strategy for building religious expertise and future faith-based leadership density within a school community. It is pleasing to see that there is some recent movement in this direction.

Generational change is a fact, as is the changing face of Australia. In Australia the cultural bedrock of unifying beliefs and norms is no longer what it once was. However, we have much to hope for in the 20 per cent of Australians who identified as Catholic in the 2021 census. In our schools and in our classes we can find common ground, goodwill and dialogue within the diversity of our demographic. We can do this as we boldly take the next chapter of our story in Catholic education into the unfolding landscape of the 21st century.

## Reflection

1. How do you think we can create schools where a meaningful Catholic encounter for students takes place?
2. To what extent do you think witness is important in imparting an effective curriculum and/or building a compassionate community of faith?
3. What changes in views about religion and spirituality have you experienced since you left school? How do you view the impact of secularisation on religious practice in Australia?
4. What do you see as the 'currents of the time' that are influencing young people in our Catholic schools?
5. What is needed from Catholic leadership in the education sector?
6. Do we educate for faith or for life? Should one or other of these have primacy in a faith-based school?
7. How do you think we can take the next chapter of Catholic education into the future?

## Contents

**Part 1 Witness**    1
Chapter 1:    Growing Up in Kew – Ann    3
Chapter 2:    Growing Up in Ballarat – Bernadette    19
Chapter 3:    Teenage Years – Ann    29
Chapter 4:    Teenage Years – Bernadette    42

**Part 2 Specialist**    55
Chapter 5:    University Days and Early Teaching – Bernadette    57
Chapter 6:    University Days and Early Teaching – Ann    67

**Part 3 Moderator**    83
Chapter 7:    Changing Landscape    84
Chapter 8:    Today's Context and its Implications    101
Chapter 9:    Current Issues    143
Chapter 10:    Future Prospects    157
Chapter 11:    Summary    179
Chapter 12:    Concluding Thoughts    183

Acknowledgements    196
Appendix 1    197
Appendix 2    199
Glossary    203

# Part 1

# witness

The religious educator is someone who can and must bear witness to the traditions to which s/he has derived her/his own religious/ideological identity (Pollefeyt, 2008, p. 8).

Figure 1.1: Ann's parents, James and Barbara O'Neill, on their wedding day 22nd December 1956

## CHAPTER ONE
# Growing Up in Kew
## – Ann

*The past is a foreign country: they do things differently there.*
L.P Hartley, *The Go-Between* (1953)

I was born into the Catholic faith with its strong Irish strain and the heavy incense of history through O'Neill, Kavanagh, Hutchinson and Byrnes genealogy. My parents had met in Melbourne. It was a doctor-nurse romance at St Vincent's Hospital and they became engaged here. As was the thing in those days, my father went overseas to Edinburgh to further his studies and a year later my mother followed him. They married at St Peter's Morningside and a neat ten months later (October 1957) I was born in the George Eliot Memorial Hospital in Nuneaton, Warwickshire. I have only recently come into possession (after 64 years) of my original baptismal certificate, mislaid in the labyrinth of the family history archive. This confirms I was baptised in the local church of Our Lady of the Angels when I was two months old, shortly before my parents took the sea journey home to Melbourne.

I cannot remember much of my early years, but I was to become the oldest of seven siblings. My life revolved around the family and helping, or hindering, my mother as she looked after the babies. My growing faith was quite simply the air I breathed. I was born into a Catholic cosmology and have never doubted its rightness or influence on me. That does not mean I have not questioned and wondered and prayed about some things over time. But as I write this now, my faith is part of my identity, not in a holier-than-thou way, but in a way that is sown deeply; so it was a morning offering for another day, prayers at bedtime and the strong belief in guardian angels and a growing understanding of God who loved me and my family. With a devout grandmother to pick up any lapses occasioned by the household chaos of school, kinder, meals, laundry, the familial fracas of those large Catholic families, my faith was confirmed in the minutiae of my daily life.

My school days were happy. I started at my mother's *alma mater*, Genazzano Convent, a day and boarding school established in 1889 by the Faithful Companions of Jesus (fcJ). In 1963 I was ready at six to be a big girl. I was so excited that first day, with my crimson velvet hat wedged on, my indoor out-door shoes packed, my polka dot pinny ready to cover my tunic during art lessons, my lunchbox named and packed with sandwiches and my blazer with its Cash's name tag sewn sturdily on the inside. My mother was sent home in tears when Reverend Mother Euphemia King fcJ told her in no uncertain words that I would be just fine. I ran into the playground of the junior school and was ready to make friends straight away. And I did – and I still have those friends half a century later!

The teachers, religious and lay, knew their subject and they knew me. I was 'named and known'. I was marvellously encouraged with fair-minded feedback that enabled me to improve and to later see myself as someone who could do well if I worked hard. Together with the academic rigours of school life, there was always the sacred tapestry being woven into my soul. The Catholic mould was set quite firmly and I embraced it all with a glad heart and open and unquestioning ways.

I was a 'biddable' student, perhaps something of a teacher-pleaser, but I knew my prayers and my catechism. Learning by heart was the order of the day and my skills in rote and recitation for spelling and tables stood me in good stead. I knew that God made me because

Figure 1.2: Genazzano school photo, 1969 – Ann (back row) with her sisters, Geraldine and Fiona.

he loved me. Although I can now see this was an indoctrination of sorts, there was something sweet in the happy burble of a class full of students who knew the answers to the catechism. Just to keep us on our toes, Mother would occasionally ask an individual to recite an answer. My little heart knew then those momentary clutchings of fear before the right answer tumbled out. As Campion (1987, p. 146) notes, the rhythm of the catechism answers served as a mnemonic device because the catechism had to be remembered. I can recall how we tested each other in the playground before class, checking that we were word-perfect. A generation of Catholics knew by heart the following:

Q: Why did God make us?
A: God made us to know, love and serve Him here on earth; and to see and enjoy Him forever in Heaven.

I loved the romance of the dusky chapel with its flickering votive candles, its gladioli floral offerings, its beeswaxed pews, its fug of incense and hushed gloom. We trooped across the garden, not talking, but shuffling in quietly, knowing this was God's house and we had to be on our best behaviour. No squirming in our seats, no laughing or coughing, just eyes cast down in prayer and standing and sitting as required. Plaster statues of Our Lady and St Joseph, now quietly archived, stood guard by the altar. The golden tabernacle was the centre point of worship. We heard about the Host and how precious it was and the glowing red light that said that God was home.

I loved the hymns and processions and statues and saints' days, and the treats from Reverend Mother on her birthday as we curtsied to her and presented floral tributes. I loved the pictures of Our Lady and the angels and the made-up stories about the black-habited nuns and the parts of the convent that were out of bounds behind heavy oak doors. We knew there were hierarchies and that dear

Mother Flavia Selleck fcJ, who cleaned out the bins and taught us needlework, was on the lowest rung. She was the patient soul who uncomplainingly finished off our knitting as we completed our plain and purl *hug-me-tights* for poor babies – our first understanding of doing something for others beyond the family. We wondered what really happened in the refectories after the boarders, big bold girls from country Victoria, had gone to bed and if they ever saw the sisters out of their habits. Did the sisters even have hair? What were their real names? Did they have strange rituals performed away from the apparent ordinariness of our school day?

I loved the dash of mystery as we talked about saints and spectres and the Grey Lady who reputedly stalked the corridors at night. We were in thrall with these stories that kept us both entertained and compliant. No one wanted to be sent to Reverend Mother because they had been naughty, and getting an order mark for a minor infraction lost points for the House to which you belonged. You could also gain points, but the fear of an order, deportment or a punctuality mark was such an ignominy that we were never late, always clean and tidy, and never answered back. No one wanted to be called a hoyden, a word dripping with unseemly qualities. Silence marks were given if we were found talking. In fact, they were bestowed quite liberally in an era where the maxim 'empty vessels make the most sound' was oft repeated. This proverb may have stifled loquaciousness briefly, but it could never really stop the natural talkativeness of groups of girls. Initiative was not encouraged in those big classes where we did our work in exercise books, wrote out a hundred lines if one member of the class had been unruly, and learned Maths with the latest invention, Cuisenaire Rods.

I loved school and flourished, but I know for some there were wounds sown because they were humiliated in those days of standing in the corner. I witnessed the awful struggles of the dyslexic students who tried to read words they could not decipher. These were the days of 'owning up', the examination of conscience and being 'on your honour'. 'Bold' girls got into trouble with the teacher for talking back and showing initiative or spark. The rest of us got on uncomplainingly with our worksheets and neat cursive copying from the blackboard.

My childhood piety was of the unquestioning kind, seasoned by the rhythm of the rosary, the regular confession of venial sins and the stories of the saints. These sainted lives became the fabric of a faith populated by the mysterious, the martyred and the mystical. My mother possessed a tiny silver-encased relic of St Maria Goretti, the patron saint of girls, and I would gaze at it with a mixture of curiosity and alarm, drawn into another realm of story, worlds away from Dick and Jane and the adventures of the Secret Seven.

At school we would walk across to the grotto where Our Lady stood in mystical visitation in front of the young Bernadette and say a prayer for the class of 1931 who had raised the funds to build it. I came to understand the concept of the Trinity by hearing of St Patrick's use of the shamrock as a teaching tool and could ever see him with his shillelagh as his staff as he converted pagans. I could not name the numinous, but it was all around me as the nuns taught me about the men and women whose lives were committed to God. Jesus was the obedient son and the Holy Ghost was the breath of goodness. In my childish imaginings, he was something like *Casper the Friendly Ghost*, a cartoon character seen on television when we were allowed to watch the small black and white TV on the back porch. I saw and experienced the FCJ sisters' devotion and kindness and love, a certain gentleness of demeanour, and only occasionally did they become admonitory or angry, pushed as they must have been by class sizes in excess of forty and sometimes only minimal teacher training.

Prayer punctuated our days, small swellings of gratitude or

Figure 1.3: Ann's First Communion Day in 1964

praise, or sometimes just the vague wonderings and daydreams of the childish mind as it approached the idea of God. We recited the Morning Offering as soon as we were out of bed. This set us up for the day as we donned our frumpy grey uniforms and walked to school early so we had plenty of time to play or read. The Angelus bell rang out at midday, gladly swung by the child who had been chosen for this important job that got them out of class. It split our day in two and was always the happy harbinger of lunchtime and an hour to ourselves. In this time we would play in the fairy garden, or run around squealing, playing chasey, or skip, or play ball games.

Before bed we would kneel and pray:

*Now I lay me down to sleep,*
*I pray the Lord my soul to keep.*
*If I should die before I wake,*
*I pray the Lord my soul to take.*

Sometimes we were allowed to say this in bed, just before our good-night kiss and lights out. Looking back it seems somewhat spooky, but for us it was what we did, closing the day with God and knowing that our guardian angels were with us, even in slumber. Between times, our supplication to the saints depended on their stories – the grislier the better. There was no room for the neat deaths of gentle expiration or graced last moments or celestial dormition. Stories of scourging and gouging and lions' dens and glorious unbowed, unflinching martyrdom took hold. This was faith of the lion-hearted variety. I loved it from the safety of my own unchallenged freedom to believe. On the asphalt at playtime, we swapped holy pictures like footy cards, drank little milk triangles and began to understand that everyone else we knew believed and behaved pretty much as we did in those days of mantillas and missals.

By Grade Two I was ready for the sacrament of First Holy

Communion. We children were made to understand that this was a really big step in our faith journey. The theology of transubstantiation was too hard to imagine for our tiny trusting minds, but we accepted this miracle in an aura of wonder and mystery. I still have the black-and-white photo of that day at the Genazzano chapel – me a buck-toothed, freckled, cheerful child of God, perkily pious in my white dress and veil. I remember the breakfast afterwards with the jelly cream slices that were a treat for a child who had plain milk biscuits at home. I know that many of us were nervous about our teeth and tongues as the importance of the reception of the Host had been drilled into us. I still possess the certificate with its beautiful calligraphy in gold painstakingly worked on by one of the FCJ sisters who did this for each child in the class.

Confession was a bit of a scary sacrament in the old days. Reconciliation today has a much more restorative and holistic feeling about it. My mother would pile us into the car, a motley group of small sinners, and take us to church to confess to Father behind the curtained grille the dobbing, fibbing, pinching (sisters, and someone else's prized purple Derwent pencil) and impure thoughts that seemed to cover my eight-year-old transgressions. Everything was on my conscience. Small excusable failings were transmogrified into giant moral lapses. Sometimes I had to invent some generic sinfulness if the litany of failings did not seem quite long enough. They may have been a small swag of suburban venalities, but they represented SIN and that was scary. The one-size-fits-all shame of being rude to my parents was a useful last minute addition in exchange for absolution. After a short penance of three *Hail Marys* and a *Glory Be* I felt good with God again.

For Confirmation, I took Barbara, my mother's name, because I loved her and because Saint Barbara had an exotic life and a defiant and gruesome end. Amongst my peers there were lots of Marys and Margarets and Thereses and Bernadettes, so I was also happy that 'Barbara' was a bit different and not one of the usual sanctified suspects. This sacrament was a statement that I was fully cognisant of what I was doing. My faith was no longer simply inherited. I was making a confirmed choice to be a Catholic. Looking back, I may have simply been that 'biddable' child (willing to do what was asked, obedient and docile). I know I was a believing child and happy to follow through the sacramental journey mapped out for me. As a child of the late 1950s I have never rescinded the choices made for me. In fact I am grateful for the many blessings of faith I have encountered thus far in my life.

My mother was devoted to St Gerard Majella, the patron saint of expectant mothers. There were frequent invocations to Saint Anthony for lost or mislaid domestic items or the car keys. On those frantic days when twenty-four hours coping with the needs of six children under ten was not nearly enough, St Jude, hope of the hopeless, was sent an urgent word.

Much of my childhood faith was learned through my grandmother. She would often respond with the phrases 'Saints alive' or 'Saints preserve us' or 'Jesus, Mary and Joseph' when her usually inexhaustible patience had been sorely tried. She really did have the patience of a saint. She loved the cavalcade of Catholic saints and was rather pleased that she lived just opposite Raheen, Archbishop Mannix's residence in Kew, and that the enclosed Carmelite monastery was at the end of her street. Campion College backed onto her property and many a time as I helped her with her garden I would hear the thwack of a tennis ball as seminarians let off steam. She was spoilt for choice on a Sunday as she could go to the Jesuits or down Studley Park Road to the Pallottines for Mass, or make the longer journey to Sacred Heart just beyond the junction, with a granddaughter, usually me, in tow.

We children would tag behind my mother as she visited the Redemptorist Monastery in Kew. Desperate to get outside and play chasey, four, five or six of us were always distracted as we prayed and my mother offered her domestic load up to God. Sometimes we would stop off at Sacred Heart, Our Lady of Good Counsel in Deepdene, or St Anthony's in Hawthorn, in those days when the doors to churches were open for us to 'pay a visit'. My father ensured we all went to Mass and doled out threepence for the plate and quelled any sibling shuffling in the pew. We eyed off other big families and waited for the blessed release from the Latin Mass we did not understand. Outside the church our parents talked and my father went home to read *The Advocate*, think about writing a letter to the editor, and watch Bob Santamaria's *Point of View*. He did not watch *World Of Sport* after this, but I know that for many Catholic families, who liked a bet on the horses or watched the VFL, this was mandatory viewing before sitting down to the Sunday roast with a voluble saying of grace before the meal.

My father's faith was practical. It was he who sent money to the missions in India, campaigned for Right to Life, wrote letters to priests and politicians and premiers. It was he who did honorary work at hospitals and always had a good word for the Sisters of Charity. He admired the Christian Brothers who had bothered with a working-class boy, and provided him with a scholarship, so he could eventually graduate from St Kevin's and study medicine at The University of Melbourne. My father was bookish and dutiful, a plain-spoken man doing his best and faithful to the Church all his days. I still have the white bust of Archbishop Daniel Mannix that was on his desk. This stood as a reminder of this renowned prelate and his anti-conscription stance in 1917 in opposition to Prime Minister Billy Hughes. This was when Archbishop Mannix famously said, 'Australia first, Empire second' (*The Argus*, letters to the editor, 8 November 1917). The bust was also a reminder of the Archbishop's redoubtable leadership of the Melbourne tribe who mourned his passing at 99 years of age in 1963.

My grandmother taught me the mysteries of the rosary and gave me tuppence to light candles in the Ladye Chapel at St Francis' in the city. Those stubby little candles represented my messy efforts at prayer; a bit of wheedling, some thanks and praise, an attempt at deal-making about homework and a pious Amen. Sometimes my prayers were as stubby and faltering as those small wax sticks because I was transfixed by the beautiful ceiling and stained-glass windows, and the other people murmuring and shuffling in this sacred space. When I stayed overnight at my grandmother's home, we would always recite the rosary; the perfect enunciation of the first few Hail Marys gradually slipping away from the 'blessed art thou amongst women' to what Malachy McCourt notes as 'a monk swimming'. In the second bedroom I would settle under a giant eiderdown quilt with a picture of the Sacred Heart above my head. My grandmother would come in to kiss me goodnight and we'd go through the 'God Bless' litany and list. Sometimes my order of petition would change depending on sibling stoushes, but hers invariably stayed the same.

The iconography of devotion decorated my grandmother's home – crucifixes, a statue of the Infant of Prague, scapulars, medals, holy pictures and other saintly ephemera. Like many, she had a great fondness for St Thérèse of Lisieux, the Carmelite champion of The Little Way, her everyday mode of holiness illuminated in small gestures rather than grand and sweeping public piety. This had great appeal to the people in the pews who understood the reality of the holy in the humdrum as they lived quiet, decent, faithful lives. She also possessed a copy of Feruzzi's *Madonnina* which decorated many walls in Catholic homes. On the Sunday sojourns to Sacred Heart she would meet her bridge and bowling friends. She would don an armoury of marcasite, a dab of Apple Blossom and her Queen Mother hat, whilst I would trail happily behind her up the aisle to secure a pew close to the altar. She made frequent novenas and dutifully saved stamps for the missions, prayed for the unbaptised infants doomed

Figure 1.4: Madonnina (Ferruzzi, 1897)

to Limbo, and put her widow's mite on the collection plate.

We speak often of our fathers in faith. But in the home, it is the mother who makes sure prayers are said. It is the mother whose active example hands on the faith. It is the mother who organises the donations, who puts herself down for the church or tuck-shop roster, who hears the catechism answers, who insists on grace before meals when ravenous children gather around the kitchen table. For children, a mother's actions and devotions, her daily attitude to God in her life, are discernible by her children before they can fully comprehend their own religious heritage, before they can grasp God for themselves. She is the first educator in faith.

So, this is the holy-picture past of growing up Catholic in Melbourne. It was a time when the parish priest pontificated and the congregation took their lead from the local Archbishop. It was a church whose members displayed features of what Fowler (1981) would call a Mythic-Literal faith (Stage 2) or, at least, a Synthetic-Conventional Faith (Stage 3), an unexamined, non-analytical faith, with members lacking the ability or will to critically reflect on their belief system.

There was almost universal, unquestioning respect for the moral authority and the Magisterium of the Church. It was a time of compliance and obedience before the breath of new life occasioned by Vatican II; this *aggiornamento* or the bringing up to date of the Church in response to the changes and challenges of a new age. Some would say that it was a simpler time where only anointed voices were heard and those in the pews were subordinate and mostly happily so. However, the voice of the Church was unequivocally male. Catholics knew who they were and complied with the practices and rituals of belonging and enjoyed a particular solidarity and homogeneity. As Edmund Campion notes (1987, p. 142) the majority of Catholics were the product of the parish school and the religion they imbibed there became the standard and foundation of whatever else followed.

It was the time of large parishes, bulging primary schools with fee reductions for the second and further siblings, and the unselfish and arduous work undertaken by the religious orders who educated Catholic children. It was a time of classes that may have consisted of fifty students or more who dared not misbehave, answer back or propose another point of view. It was a time when Lent was for 'giving up' lollies and cakes, a minor mortification for students who otherwise lived on the meat and three veg staple of many families, except, of course, for fish on Friday. It was a time when belief was like breathing and supporting overseas missionary activity through the Propagation of the Faith was routine and active. In the 1950s, 95 per cent of the teaching staff in Australian Catholic schools were religious (Campion, p. 235), so in the 1960s this number was still very high. Respect for those consecrated to religious life was pervasive and what *Mother, Father* or *Brother* said at school was gospel!

Today, the world looks very different. Times change and the voice of the people of God asks for a new way, a way of being in the Church that is authentic for this age. That is where we stand now, looking ahead to reshape the Church as fit for its purpose as it learns to live again the message of Jesus of Nazareth in an increasingly secular, pluralist world.

## References

Campion, Edmund, *Australian Catholics,* Viking, Ringwood, 1987.

Hartley, LP, *The Go-Between,* Hamish Hamilton, 1953.

Fowler, JW, *Stages in Faith: The Psychology of Human Development and the Quest for Meaning*, Harper & Row, New York, 1981.

## Reflection

1. What are the standout events, memories and people that have influenced you on your journey to faith?
2. Do you have memories of collective occasions or sacramental celebrations where worshipping in community was prioritised?
3. What rituals, artefacts and books do you recall growing up with?
4. Have we lost a sense of belonging and identity over the years? If so, why? And how do you think this has come about?
5. Childhood years are formative for many life preferences. Did your faith take hold then? Has it changed through experience? What are your feelings towards the institution that is the Catholic Church today?

## CHAPTER TWO
## Growing Up in Ballarat – Bernadette

*Those were the days, my friend, we thought they'd never end …*
Mary Hopkins, 1968

This story begins 65 years ago in the regional city of Ballarat on a very hot January day in 1957. I have very fond memories of growing up in Ballarat, despite the fact that alongside hot summers it had extremely cold winters that gave me chilblains – which I have never had since! At that time, Ballarat had a population of about 60,000 and was much more a country town than it is today. Green rattler trams dominated the main street, Sturt Street. Myers was the only major department store, and a horse and cart delivered our bottles of milk every day, at least when I was very young. There were no universities as there are today and the idea of a café had not yet surfaced. In fact, the idea of eating out or having a coffee was foreign to this world.

I was the eldest child of Margaret and Des Harty who would go on to have six children. My dad was a local boy, very devoted to his mother who had lost her husband when dad was a child and had two older sisters who lived in Adelaide and Melbourne. My mother, on the other hand, had grown up in the small dairy farming hamlet of Newry, near Maffra in Gippsland, the fourth child of a family of six. She had trained in Melbourne as a hairdresser but came to Ballarat to keep company with her eldest brother, Fr William Dwyer, a diocesan priest who was posted there. This is where she met my dad at a local Young Christian Workers' dance. These dances were a regular feature of parish life in those days, and many a romance began on those old church hall floors!

My parents were married on 11 February 1956, which is known in the Catholic calendar as the Feast of Our Lady of Lourdes. This commemorates the miracle of the apparition of Our Lady to the young peasant girl Bernadette Soubirous that occurred in Lourdes, France, on this date in 1858. I was born eleven months later and named Bernadette Mary. This was partly because of the wedding date, but also the fact that one of my mum's favourite cousins was Sr Bernadette, a Sister of Charity. Bernadette is a quintessential Catholic name and I have had a mixed relationship with it over the years. I like that it is not all that common, especially these days, but the fact that it automatically labels you as a Catholic – or, at least of Catholic origins – was not always something I wanted. These days, I just spend most of my time spelling it out if for people in shops and other places! I was baptised two weeks later, as was the custom in those traditional Catholic days. In fact, this was considered rather late to do this. Many babies were baptised within a week of their birth as there was a fear that if a child died unbaptised, they would go to a place called Limbo on the borders of heaven. This is a Catholic teaching that has slowly slid into the background and was finally discounted as a formal teaching by Pope Benedict in 1992. However, at this time of my infancy no parent wanted to risk their baby ending up there! There were stories of parents desperately phoning a priest to come to their sick new baby to baptise them lest they die and go into Limbo. My baptism was possibly delayed a little as it might have been a question of availability as I was baptised by my Uncle Bill who would have had many calls and commitments on his time. I imagine that a two-week delay would have been quite a trial for my parents!

I have small pockets of memories of those early days, including

Figure 2.1: Wedding of Bernadette's parents – Margaret Dwyer and Des Harty, 11 February 1956

Figure 2.2: Guardian Angel picture that hung above my bed.

a vivid memory of the large oval picture of what was called the Guardian Angel which hung above my bed. There were two small children, a boy and a girl, with the angel who had her hands extended over the children as they stepped forward. I do not remember being afraid of this image, but rather having a certain sense of comfort and protection. Related to this was the Guardian Angel prayer that my young brother and I were taught to say every morning:

> O Angel of God, my guardian dear,
> To whom God's love commits me here
> Ever this day, be at my side,
> To light and guard, to rule and guide,
> Amen.

In those days, there were prayers for every occasion, many contained in small prayer-books. The idea of spontaneous or meditative prayer was not even considered. Every night we would say a prayer with my mother to bless each member of the family and to make us a good boy or good girl. I have memories of my mother each morning kneeling by her bed to say her own prayers, even when she was in her eighties. Similar to Ann's mother, mine always had a picture in her kitchen of St Jude, hope of the hopeless, and also one of St Gerard Majella, patron saint of mothers. My mother was very fond of these two saints and I imagine turned to them frequently as she raised six lively children.

I have early memories of going with Mum and Dad to St Patrick's Cathedral for Mass, all dressed in my Sunday best with a little boater hat. We usually sat near the front of this large church so that I could see. I could only understand the sermon as everything else was in Latin. My parents each had a missal, a small book that had Latin on one side of the page and English on the other. Inserted in the missal were holy cards of different saints or Mary or the Sacred Heart of

Figure 2.3: Berndadette – early days of school

Jesus, often in remembrance of family members who had died.

I have memories of the altar servers – all male – putting down the cloths over the altar rail and then parishioners filing up to the altar rails, kneeling down and receiving communion on their tongues. The priest climbed the steps in the pulpit to stand high above us – reflective of the status that priests had in these days – and mostly admonished his flock about the evil allure of hell! At other times there was Benediction where the host was put by the priest into a monstrance (a special vessel for the occasion), surrounded by lots of candles and incense. This was a pre-Vatican II Church with lots of tradition but unfortunately a fortress mentality that no-one dared to question. However, this was soon to change as I got just a little older.

Other early memories include riding around the street in which I lived on my small bicycle to visit my neighbourhood friends. These included a lovely older lady, Mrs Coffey, and a girl who was several years older than me called Jeanette who I adored, having no-one else around my own age to play with. The street was relatively quiet. There was a sense of safety back in the 1950s and early 1960s that we seem to have lost today. I believe this early sense of neighbourhood has stayed with me over the years and neighbourliness/community remains an important part of who I am today.

I started school at Loreto College, Dawson St at the tender age of four! There were not many kindergartens at this time and I was getting restless at home so Mum and Dad thought it best for me to start school. I remember my Dad taking me by the hand to the imposing front iron gates of the school. We would wait for my teacher, Sr André, to come over and take my hand so that I would reluctantly let go of my Dad's hand. I was a very shy child and it took a long time for me to walk in more confidently! The Loreto and most other nuns at this time wore long black serge habits, tied with a rope and cross, with a black veil and wimple that covered everything but the face. They were strange creatures to little four and

Figure 2.4: Pioneer Loreto sisters, Loreto Province Archives, Australia & South East Asia

Figure 2.5: Benadette's First Communion, October 1963

five year olds. We loved Sr André, but the head nun and some of the older nuns were quite fearsome. We wondered if they had hair and did they really eat normally? The Loreto nuns had as their founder, Mary Ward. Mary began the Loreto Order, in Yorkshire, England in 1609, at a time when nuns were cloistered. Mary wanted her nuns to be 'contemplatives in action' combining a life of prayer with active missions in schools, drawing on the spirituality of her contemporary, St Ignatius of Loyola. She believed that women religious could lead such a life, just as the Jesuits did, and that women in time would do great things.

Religion played a significant part of school life in those days. Every first Thursday of the month we would walk in a long line of pairs down Dawson St and across Sturt St to St Patrick's Cathedral for confession (for those who had made their first confession). We were very focused on the confessional boxes and the wooden pews we sat on whilst waiting for our turn to go inside. It was very dark inside and you waited for the priest to draw open the curtain so you could begin your confession. As a young child there was not much you could say – I teased my brothers and sisters, I did not help my Mum with the dishes, I told a lie! We rehearsed these on our walk down Dawson St and the list never varied much. Then, on the next day, the first Friday of the month, we walked back to the Cathedral for Mass. This practice was linked to a belief that 'Jesus had promised a seventeenth century nun that everyone receiving Communion on the first Friday of nine consecutive months would not die in sin' (Campion, 1998, p. 144). I somehow do not think we did much school work in the first week of every month!

My First Communion was in Grade 2, unlike today when it is often Grade 4. This was a big occasion involving getting a white dress – my Mum made mine – and a white veil. We prepared every day in school, learning how to take communion on the tongue and going over to the Cathedral to practice where to stand. I cannot remember much more about that day except that it was on the Feast of Christ the King in October at about 8.00 am and then we had hard-boiled eggs and sandwiches for breakfast, sitting in a long row in the Cathedral hall. We were hungry little communicants as in those days you could not eat from an hour before Mass! I would often feel faint in Mass because of this.

Processions were a big part of pre-Vatican II life. Once we had made our First Communion, in the following year we were often invited to be part of various religious processions that occurred around the oval at the Christian Brothers' school, St Patrick's College. The most important were the Feast of Corpus Christi and the Feast of Christ the King. We had to dress up in our white dresses and veils, which we liked doing, and bring a bag filled with rose petals. We would then walk in front of the Bishop who walked under a canopy holding the host in a monstrance. The routine with the rose petals that was instilled in us was, 'Take, kiss and follow through.' Then we flung them gracefully on the ground as we processed. Other processions occurred at school such as on the May 1 which was the start of what was considered as Mary's month. The procession this time involved each class carrying a basket of flowers around the yard and then moving into the hall where a statue of Mary was crowned with flowers, and all the baskets placed at her feet. We sang songs such as 'Oh Mary, we crown thee with blossoms today, queen of the angels and queen of the May!'

As mentioned in the previous chapter, this was a very traditional unquestioning Church in which I spent my early years. It was a secure world, but with inflexible rules, such as never missing Mass on Sunday, ladies always wearing a hat in church (thanks St Paul!) and not eating meat on Fridays. With our Mythic-Literal or Synthetic-Conventional faith (Fowler, 1981), no-one dared to question these rather dubious practices but instead we firmly believed that not adhering to them would put us into a state of mortal sin! Most every aspect of life was linked with the Catholic Church and this Church only – heaven forbid going into the Presbyterian Church close to the school or the Church of England in Sturt St! But by the time I was in about Grade 3, as you will see in the following chapters, the church began to change, with Pope John XXIII calling the Second Vatican Council which ran from 1962 to 1965. Life and school became quite different.

## References

Campion, E, *Australian Catholics*, Penguin Books, 1988.

Fowler, JW, (1981), *Stages in Faith: The Psychology of Human Development and the Quest for Meaning*, Harper & Row, New York, 1981.

## Reflection

1. What do you think were the advantages of living in a religious environment in the 1950s and 1960s?
2. What were the limitations and disadvantages?
3. Have we lost anything from the past?
4. What aspects of Bernadette's experiences can you identify with?

## CHAPTER THREE
## Teenage Years – Ann

*Spirit of God in the clear running water*
*Blowing to greatness the trees on the hill*
*Spirit of God in the finger of morning*
*Fill the Earth, bring it to birth*
*And blow where you will*
*Blow, blow, blow 'til I be*
*But the breath of the Spirit blowing in me.*
Bob Rowe

I remember the 14th of February 1966, etched as it was so clearly into the national consciousness, with the catchy *Click go the Shears* tune heralding the introduction of decimal currency that year. I was eight. However, even more important and defining for me was the moon landing in 1969. Soon after the event we were shuffled into the middle school hall to stare at some grainy pictures of Neil Armstrong's *one small step for man, one great leap for mankind*. Overnight the moon and some of its celestial mystery was wrenched open. The American flag placed on its lunar surface was indicative of the space race that had grown out of the Cold War. That beautiful mistress of the night skies, she of benevolent democracy and tender voyeurism with her cool lucent glow, had been conquered. And we would forever look at the waxing and waning of the moon in a different light.

I was still at Genazzano as my teen years began, and like all Catholic schools it had a rich heritage. The history and tradition of the school began to grow on me in the way of what used to be known as 'school spirit'. We had been used to the sisters in their black habits for winter and their white ones for summer so to see them in civvies was a shock. Vatican II had thrown open the windows of the Church, letting in both a new Spirit and ameliorating some of the fustiness that had constrained the energy of the post-war generation. For the older sisters this was a radical departure and some simply refused to abandon the habit of a lifetime. Generational differences were apparent even within religious orders. The sisters dressed for practicality, not fashion, and the colour palette was initially rather dour as they became used to being seen in public without their traditional attire.

*Perfectae Caritatis* (1965) offered general principles for the adaptation and renewal of apostolic life to the changed conditions of the time. A return to the source of the original spirit of the various religious institutes was recommended so that each could revisit their founding stories and adapt them as they saw fit. However, it took time for the stories of the founders and foundresses to be widely told and to become a regular part of the religious education curriculum. Prior to this, Catholic students understood that those in religious life were tasked with humility, as well as poverty, chastity and obedience, and any sort of individual self-aggrandisement was antithetical to the communal imperative. Modest deprecation was the *modus operandi* of most female religious orders. Of course names and areas of contribution were acknowledged, but the exercise of individuality was frowned upon and selfless compliance and anonymity the order of the day. This reminds me of the observation that more often than not in the great swathe of human history, 'Anon' has been a woman. This was even more so in a patriarchal and hierarchical Church, with its monolithic stained-glass ceiling whereby the majority of religious sisters accepted their routine subordination. Such modesty and invisibility were seen as virtues.

For the Faithful Companions of Jesus – the Catholic order

responsible for Genazzano – 1970 was a watershed year. This was the year that the foundress, Marie Madeleine de Bengy de Bonnault d'Houët, was declared a woman of heroic virtue and given the title *Venerable*. Marie Madeleine Victoire was born in Châteauroux, France in 1781 to devout and royalist parents and was dedicated to Our Lady when she was baptised the same day in the local church of St Martial. The family motto *Bien faire et laisser dire*, which translated means 'Do what is right and do not worry what others say' was to become a guiding philosophy for this faith-filled woman who died in 1858. She had been a wife, mother and widow, a large landowner from the *ancien régime.* Her spiritual journey led her to the influence of the Jesuits when her only child boarded at the Petit Séminaire Saint-Acheul in Amiens. The family had provided refuge for priests who had fled imprisonment or worse under the French Revolution (1789-1799) during those years of civic unrest. This was when the social and economic inequalities of the urban poor and the regional peasantry ignited conflict across the country and a denunciation of the rule of Church and monarchy.

As a young woman, Marie Madeleine had ministered to the poor in Issoudun and saw how hard life was for those with few means and a lack of opportunity for social mobility through the power of education. From the outset, she understood that her faith and her privilege demanded that she work for those who did not have the advantages into which she was born. In 1820, Marie Madeleine founded the Society of the Faithful Companions of Jesus, in recognition of those women who stood at the foot of the cross as Jesus of Nazareth died and who understood both his 'I thirst' and the thirst in the world for salvation. She aimed to improve the lives of girls and women whom she saw as spiritually and educationally impoverished and to give them opportunities and aspirations beyond which their birth circumstances may have destined for them. During her lifetime, Marie Madeleine founded schools in England, Ireland

and the continent. She was known to remind her teaching staff that every child with whom they interacted represented the child Jesus and was therefore deserving of love – and patience.

The story of the Faithful Companions of Jesus in Australia began in 1882. In response to a plea from Father Dalton SJ, they came to provide a much-missed Catholic education for the young colonists in Victoria. The Archbishop of Melbourne, Dr James Goold, was very pleased that 'the twelve apostles' had arrived to provide a quality education for the young faithful. The sisters were greeted with rousing cordiality as they stepped off the boat from Liverpool after a six-week sea journey. They were at work teaching the next week in Richmond, where Vaucluse FCJ Convent was established a few years later. In 1889 a community of eight nuns, under the guidance of Mother Stanislaus Stock fcJ, moved into 'Woodlands' in Kew and thus began the Genazzano school story.

The early years of faith education in Australia were distinctively Irish in character and conviction. Edmund Campion (1987, p. 4) makes this point eloquently when he speaks of the Irish convicts who carried the faith to this country and kept it alive, even when they did not have Catholic clergy with them on a consistent basis, as follows:

> ... without the ministrations of the priests, the Catholic faith survived in colonial Australia as a poem that gave life meaning and respite. It was a view of the world enabling one to sustain the present and hope for the future. It was also a folk culture, a bond of loyalty to one's fellows. The tenacity of this layman's religion cannot be measured by attendance at Mass or financial contributions to the clergy. Yet what evidence there is points to the hardiness of this colonial transplant of the Catholic faith from Ireland.

Thus the Irish element in the growth of Australian Catholicism was there from the arrival of the First Fleet. They were partisan, anti-Protestant and anti-British, especially because of the pauperisation and their consequent landlessness in their own homeland. The Irish were fiercely tribal and the faith of the fathers took root and flourished, despite the challenges it faced, not least of which was establishing the sector that secured a Catholic education in the faith with its attendant popular cultural associations.

The FCJ spirit was premised on the Constitutions of the Society of Jesus and Ignatian spirituality. *La douceur*, or gentleness, was one of the animating gifts of this distinctive charism as Marie Madeleine undertook her mission to the poor and uneducated. She was a contemporary of St Madeleine-Sophie Barat, the foundress of The Society of the Sacred Heart, who had been keen to have Marie Madeleine join her order. However, Marie Madeleine sought a different way to exercise her spiritual gifts and knew that God had a special plan for her. Both Marie Madeleine and Mary Ward, the English foundress of the Institute of the Blessed Virgin, the Loreto Sisters of whom Bernadette speaks, expressed the desire to be *une jesuitesse*. The spirituality embodied in the Ignatian notion of *contemplatives in action* was and is foundational to the charism of the Society of The Faithful Companions of Jesus.

Over time, many teaching orders were able to adapt and implement, as was particular to their charism and characteristics, 'the Church's undertaking and aims in matters biblical, liturgical, dogmatic, pastoral, ecumenical, missionary and social' (PC 2.C.) This recognition of individual charismatic identity forged new affection for congregational founding stories and a refreshing and retelling of them for contemporary understanding and resonance. Thus, an order's charismatic patrimony could become part of the continuing community experience and ongoing story.

Also in 1970, Pope Paul VI was the first pope to visit Australia when he touched down in Sydney for three days. I cannot remember this, although I do remember pictures of him in the classrooms of our day. For Melbourne and Victorian Catholics, the 1973 Eucharistic Congress was a feat of both logistics and the brokering of new ecumenical dialogue in a spirit of renewal. This was the outgrowth of the *Unitatis Redintegratio* (1964), the decree on Ecumenism which aimed at both reading the signs of the times, and the restoration of Christian unity with the *separated brethren* of other traditions (a reconciliation through dialogue with the other Christian churches). Similarly, as the last chapter described, getting 97,000 Catholic school children for the Children's Liturgy at the MCG was, at that time, the largest peace-time exercise in public transportation in Australia. The Congress was opened by Cardinal Lawrence Sheehan from Baltimore. Of particular note, this was the first time anywhere in the country that an authentic Australian Aboriginal Liturgy was enacted during a Eucharistic celebration. Present also was Karol Wojtyla who would become the beloved Pope John Paul II five years later. A photo of the future pope, modest in a black soutane and feeding kangaroos, was taken at Healesville Sanctuary. One likes to think that he was impressed with the Great South Land of the Holy Spirit of which he spoke so warmly in his later papal visit in 1986.

Ecumenical dialogue and understanding were key themes at the Congress, as well as issues of ecology and the importance of aid to developing countries. Melburnians, particularly, would know of the MCG as the sacred ground of the VFL/AFL, but on that day it became the sacred ground for all those children cheering and fluttering their white Mass books in a rousing sense of Catholic unity – like a tribal belonging. In hindsight, perhaps it was something of a last hurrah for the old days of simple piety and deference to the preaching and instruction from the pulpit.

In Melbourne in the 1970s, we began 'grooving with the times'.

Skyhooks may well have been *livin' in the seventies* in a somewhat more adventurous way than we were, but things were changing. I remember the guitar masses at St Francis Xavier's in Box Hill where we sang 'Spirit Of God' and 'To Be Alive'; some songs more folk-troubadour and others with a bit more rock 'n' roll in them. The Medical Mission Sisters and Ray Repp were the go-to for the younger Church attendee. We still sang 'Soul of My Saviour' and 'Hail Queen of Heaven' on more formal liturgical occasions. One hymn from my childhood that still echoes for me is 'We Stand for God', a hymn composed for the 1953 Eucharistic Congress. With its anthemic boldness, this was a hymn I rather liked as something of a Crusader child. (Here I am referring to the abortive 1212 Crusade which originated in France and Germany, when charismatic preachers lured the faithful young with visions of being Christian soldiers who would travel to Jerusalem to wrest control of that holy city from the Muslim 'infidel'.)

Schooled as we were in marching in regimental order to the music of John Philip Sousa at house sports, I had imbibed and misinterpreted something of the adventure stories of the Crusades. I saw myself marching gloriously into heaven, banner held high, unbowed by any opposition. This, with its martial air and sense of unity, was a hymn of the Church Triumphant. For more standard fare, we relied on that other little red book, *The Living Parish Hymn Book* which contained some wonderful recessionals and processionals such as 'All Creatures of Our God and King' and 'Firmly, I Believe and Truly'. It seems to me that learning by heart really does stick as I still know those well-worn words.

Of course, Sister Janet Mead's version of 'Our Father' was a worldwide hit in 1973 adding some funkiness to the traditional hymn. During this period the musicals *Godspell, Jesus Christ Superstar* and *Joseph and the Amazing Technicolour Dreamcoat* were also being staged and later filmed. Some of the songs such as 'Day by Day, Any Dream

Will Do' and 'I Don't Know How to Love Him' became popular crossover hits. Jesus was being reimagined in the 1970s and I for one was a happy follower. I remember singing 'Day by Day' in a school talent quest – and winning! This was almost as significant to me as Reverend Mother tacitly approving my choice of Elvis' 'Crying in the Chapel' as my choice for a radio request show. Gerard Windsor in his recent book, *The Tempest-Tossed Church* ( 2018), quotes Australian writer Amanda Lohrey as noting that this refashioning of Jesus to contemporary ideologies of the 1960s and 1970s had him appear a gentle hippie in these post-Conciliar years. Certainly, I remember Cat Stevens' beautiful 'Morning has Broken', first released in 1971, being used as an entrance hymn for many 1970s school Masses.

For older parishioners, this must have been hard to adapt to as it was a Church they did not recognise. Schooled as they were in the traditional ways of responding to the priest who had effectively been the master of ceremonies at Mass, they were a compliant congregation. The people in the pews had been pious and obedient, mostly accepting Catholic doctrine as irrefutable. However, my own father, a devout, thinking man and an obstetrician who delivered 3000 Melbourne babies, had been sorely disappointed with the release of *Humanae Vitae* in 1964. This document affirmed the joy of married love but confirmed that couples could not use artificial contraception. Pope Paul VI went against the recommendation of the commission he had appointed to study this question and this led to some Catholics leaving the Church and some dissension in the clerical ranks. Previously, Australian Catholics had seen the machinations of the Labor Party Split (1955) and the Melbourne archbishop, Dr Mannix, and the Sydney archbishop, Cardinal Gilroy, disagreeing over how the faithful were to vote. Yes, the Melbourne/Sydney rivalry became partisan even within the generally cohesive and widespread practice and understanding of the faith of the fathers.

Figure 3.1: Wardell building, Genazzano Convent, early 20th century.

With the new permissions occasioned by Vatican II came a re-visioned ecclesial art and architecture. Out with Gothic gloom and in with light and bright spaces for communal worship. At Genazzano, the new chapel was realised. The original architectural drawings for the school proposed a chapel adjacent to the 1890 convent. This expansive design was devised whilst 'Marvellous' Melbourne was still in the ascendant as a result of the Victorian gold rush of the 1850s. Melbourne rivalled New York as a metropolis of energy and growth in the 1880s such was the capital ploughed into the city's coffers. However, the city's premier place in the British Empire foundered a couple of years later with financial travails that crippled the economy of the day. As a result of what has become known historically as the Boom and Bust of Melbourne, William Wardell's plans could not proceed as the FCJ Sisters were financially constrained and appeals to Archbishop Thomas Carr for material aid did not transpire. (Wardell is renowned as the Gothic revivalist architect who designed the cathedrals of St Patrick's Melbourne and St Mary's Sydney. Genazzano is the only school he is known to have designed).

The new chapel with its lovely stained-glass windows, clear sight lines and uncluttered ambiance allowed the congregation to breathe out. There was a visual decluttering of sacred interiors in these modernist designs which gave space to the congregation in the new more participatory liturgy that grew out of the changes in the universal Church.

At school, the way we did religion changed dramatically. The Christian living retreat of Year 11 and 12 became the thing for the spiritual-pastoral nurturing of the young Catholic. These weekends away in the company of priests and nuns as chaperones and supervisors were a bit about getting to know God and a bit about getting to know some boys. We were out of uniform, and into that other teenage uniform of jeans, sweaters and desert boots. Here we had 'deep and meaningfuls' – conversations that got below the surface and asked for some real discernment as to our faith lives and where they were leading us. Here we prepared our own paraliturgies, chose the readings and hymns and had a sense that we were creative participants in these communal devotions. My knowledge of Scripture, though, was scant. I knew the parables and miracles of the New Testament but my Old Testament understanding did not extend beyond Exodus, and then seemed to skip 1300 years to the Pax Romana and the gospel story. It seemed my Protestant friends were more conversant with the Good Word. I had an early interest in ecumenism and had happily gone to some Baptist camps, but, on reflection, I think I was just sounding out the difference in approaches to worship. This excursion to a more 'happy-clappy' devotional style made me more appreciative of my own less demonstrative tradition.

We continued to observe the Feast of the Assumption and Holy Days of Obligation. Our Lady was certainly front and centre in school tradition, especially Our Lady of Good Counsel whose shrine at Genazzano in Italy secured the name of the school in colonial Victoria. Genazzano is a mediaeval village and Marian pilgrimage site, almost 50 kilometres from Rome. It is the birthplace of Pope Martin V, whose election effectively ended the Western Schism of 1378–1417, a prolonged episode over papal legitimacy which had damaged the Church's institutional reputation. For many Gen students, visiting Genazzano becomes something of a personal pilgrimage later in their lives, a nod to an enduring founding story. Such stories, of saints and miracles and places of significance to a religious congregation, become the narrative of identity and connection between one generation and the next. Especially in these formative years, these stories and rituals can embed themselves deeply in the imagination and flower in faith and a certain loyalty to the school where this takes place. Bernadette and I are living examples of this.

We may well ask here, given the nature of this book's theme, whether these profoundly faith-formative episodes are still happening for our Catholic youth. Perhaps they are happening in a different way, in response to a world that is vastly different to the one in which we grew up and were formed in faith – and life. Perhaps the exuberance and spiritual optimism of World Youth Days, local and overseas immersion experiences helping the poor in a hands-on way and being in touch digitally, are growing a more global Church. A new borderlessness may well mean more compassion and outreach, more goodness, regardless of the named prompt that sets this in action.

Prayer was said at the beginning of each day, a morning offering to do our best. Religious iconography abounded and there was no mistaking that this was a Catholic school with its crucifixes, statues, large paintings and AMDG motto (*Ad Majorem Dei Gloriam; For the greater glory of God*) chalked onto classroom blackboards. On the sisters' feast days, we gave them little tributes; posies picked from the home garden, a tablet of good lavender soap, some chocolates or perhaps something handmade. We learned about the importance of dying in a 'state of grace' and 'occasions of sin'. Liturgical dancing, a more acrobatic approach to devotion with its swirling ribbons and kaleidoscopic colours, added a new dimension to the way we worshipped. 'Lord Of The Dance' was top of the pops in the hymn category in those heady years when there was a recognition that we could pray like the Whirling Dervishes of the Sufi tradition, with bodies as well as souls.

Fundraising was part of a House or class competition. We donated to Meals on Wheels, St Vincent de Paul and the House of Urchins. We Walked against Want, had dress-up days, went doorknocking for good causes and made sure small coins were put into the purple Project Compassion box at home. We manned a stall at the Maytime Fair at Xavier College and were given to understand that we should give out of our abundance and good fortune. Loving God and loving neighbours and dutifully attending Mass were the lived realities of my late teenage years. Across the globe, Liberation Theology was taking hold in South American countries, but this was yet to find its way into the RE classroom of the middle 1970s. So we graduated from school, our faith yet undented by worldly experience, almost innocents abroad, excited by what lay ahead and how our lives might change.

## References:

Campion, E, *Australian Catholics*, Viking (Penguin) Books, Ringwood, Australia, 1987.

## Reflection

1. Reflecting on your school experience, who or what do you see as influential people/ events/ places that may have been formative for you?
2. Did your Catholic school celebrate the founding story/charism? How? When? Was this animating story seamed through your whole school experience from primary to secondary?
3. Do you have a favourite hymn/ hymns? Share these and explain why they resonated for you.
4. Are there any books, films, musicals from your youth that have a God/Christian/Jesus/ redemptive theme? What about today? How would these work in the contemporary Catholic classroom?
5. Did your experience of 'church' provide comfort, a sense of social cohesion and community? If, so how?

## CHAPTER FOUR
## Teenage Years – Bernadette

*"Change in all things is sweet."*
Aristotle

There are some childhood dates involving change that are decisively etched in my memory, such as 14 February 1966, similar to Ann when Australia changed from using an imperial to a metric monetary system. My memory was perhaps aided by the catchy jingle that went with it and the new coins and notes that came into our hands. However, I cannot say the same for Vatican II (1962-1965) which, although ultimately bringing great changes in the years that followed, was not one single event, but a happening that only gradually impacted our young lives.

Having said that, the greatest change that happened for me happened overnight when I was in about Grade 3 – the nuns! We went home one afternoon, leaving behind black habited and fully veiled teachers, to return the next morning to see these same brave women dressed in knee-length light grey dresses and shorter veils showing their faces, edged by HAIR! Mind you, it was mostly only the younger nuns who did this, at least initially. The older nuns took much longer to make this change and some never did. It was a traumatic time for many of the older nuns who found their whole way of being turned upside down. Not only was their external garb changed, but nuns who had previously been called 'Mother' because of their seniority, now became 'Sister' because there was to be only one class of nuns. Many nuns who had taken religious names when they entered the Order, even masculine names such as 'Mother Michael' or 'Mother Bartholomew', reverted to their real names. The Vatican document, *Perfectae Caritatis, Decree on the Adaptation and Renewal of Religious Life*, encouraged religious orders to go back to their roots and re-discover their charism. For the Loreto Sisters, this meant reinvigorating the story and message of Mary Ward, a remarkable woman in England who believed that women could be contemplatives in action, combining a life of prayer with active ministry. Religious nuns and brothers were also permitted to adapt their lifestyle and attire for the environments they were working in.

Vatican II arose out of a new understanding of revelation, where God was now seen as present in the world and the Church charged with the duty of 'scrutinizing the signs of the times and of interpreting them in the light of the Gospel' (*Gaudium et Spes* # 4). It produced a series of documents that, as Pope St John XXIII stated, had the purpose of 'modernization of the Church after 20 centuries of life'.

Reflecting a new vision for the church of dialogue and participation, Vatican II had a profound effect on the way that Religious Education was taught in schools (Latinovic, Mannion, & Welle, 2018). The textbook, *My Way to God*, was issued and prescribed for use for Grades 1–4 in all Catholic schools in Australia in September, 1964. The text was much more child-friendly and colourful than the question/answer format of catechisms previous generations had used, and Religious Education lessons became more engaging, with more discussion, singing and interaction. This has been described as a Kerygmatic approach, based on the Greek word for *kerygma* meaning proclamation (Buchanan, 2005).

This new approach contrasted significantly with the Doctrinal approach of previous years where the focus was on doctrinal statements about belief. We also now had small copies of the Bible on our booklists as Catholics were now encouraged to engage with the Bible as their Protestant neighbours had always done. The other development was in terms of religious music. Where previously we would have sung hymns like 'Sweet Sacrament Divine' or 'Faith of our Fathers', we now were introduced to guitar songs such as 'Joy is like the Rain' and the 'Wedding Banquet' from the Medical Mission Sisters. The Belgian Dominican Singing Nun, Jeanne-Paule Marie Deckers, became very popular with her hit song *Dominique*. She performed in concerts and appeared in the Ed Sullivan Show. This would have been unheard-of and quite scandalous before Vatican II.

In terms of the parish, the Vatican document *De sacra liturgia, Commission on the Sacred Liturgy* began to have an impact on our parish church. This document called for an extensive review of worship so that all participants could be more actively involved. The first step in many parishes was constructing a new altar at the front of the sanctuary more resemblant of a table. The priest would stand there facing his congregation – a much more personal approach than standing at the back altar with his back to the congregation. Statues that abounded in pre-Vatican II churches were thinned out and new churches that were built experimented with different, more modern styles. Gradually, new liturgical texts were developed in the vernacular – the language of the people – rather than Latin.

Now the congregation would participate more actively. Where previously only male altar servers spoke the responses to the words of the priest, now all were able to say them. Added to this significant change in participation, lay people were now invited to read the first and second readings and bring up the bread and wine in the Offertory Procession. Soon after this, lay people were able to become Special Ministers, giving out communion.

There were special moments where I saw my parents go up to the lectern to read for the first time. As I grew older I got to do this too.

Figure 4.1: Sample from *My Way to God* Grade 1

Communion changed from kneeling at the altar rails and receiving the host on your tongue, to lining up and standing, holding out your hand and receiving it there, a much more hygienic practice!

At home, some practices remained the same. I have strong memories in my later primary and early secondary years of saying the family rosary after dinner each evening. My tribe of brothers and sisters and I would all be herded into the living room and we would each kneel in our allotted spot and pull out our favourite pair of rosary beads. Mine were beautiful mother-of-pearl, a gift for my First Communion. My father would then intone: 'The first Joyful Mystery, the Annunciation. Our Father …' We would sometimes take turns in leading as we got older. I remember sharp kicks in the shin if one of my brothers or sisters lost count and did 11 Hail Marys instead of 10. I cannot proclaim that saying the rosary was my favourite part of the day. I would have preferred curling up with a good book or watching something on TV. Yet in retrospect it was one of the few times in the day, apart from eating, that we did something together. And as my mother always said, 'The family that prays together, stays together!'

A particular development of the rosary that my family participated in was having a special statue of Mary coming to our home for a week. I think it was organised by the Legion of Mary, who were a lay group of women in the church. We would have family and friends join us and we would say the rosary with 'trimmings'. That meant that we would have a marathon effort of saying three rounds of the rosary – The Joyful, Sorrowful and Glorious mysteries – plus extra prayers asking different saints to pray for us. I was not all that fond of this long process, but it was worth it for the nice supper of scones and jam and cream that followed with our guests.

My later primary and secondary years were punctuated by key religious moments such as my Confirmation in Year 5, where I wore

Figure 3.2: Bernadette's Confirmation Day, 1967

a similar veil and white dress as that worn in Year 2. We also began to participate in annual school retreats. Previously a school retreat would have been a silent and passive affair of being preached to. Now there were lots of experiments with different media and activities. I remember one retreat with a young priest when I was in Year 10. He based the retreat on the book *Jonathan Livingston Seagull!* And they certainly were no longer silent!

My final two years were spent at Loreto Abbey, Mary's Mount as Loreto Dawson St only had students up to Form 4. This was a beautiful school on the banks of Lake Wendouree and my days there were some of the happiest of my schooling. Loreto Abbey, Mary's Mount was the first Loreto school in Australia, established by Mother Gonzaga Barry in 1875 at the invitation of the Bishop of Ballarat. The school's establishment was in response to the Education Act of 1872 that decreed that education needed to be 'free, compulsory and secular' (Barry, 1975). This Act ended all government funding for Catholic schools with funding not returning until the mid-1960s after the famous Goulburn Catholic Schools' Strike. This meant that the only way to keep Catholic schools open was to bring in religious nuns and brothers. The school opened on 29 September 1875 with two pupils.

We were privileged to have a beautiful chapel known as the Children's Chapel. It was built at the end of the 19th century with the ceiling painted in soft blue and sprinkled with silver stars. Part way through the building process, however, funds ran out, but the nuns were overjoyed to receive a huge bequest from the inheritance of German Countess Elizabeth Wolff-Metternich who, incognito, had been an adult boarder at the school in 1898. Whilst at the school the 22-year-old Countess had decided she wished to become a Loreto nun; however, she was encouraged by Mother Gonzaga Barry to leave the school and return home to Germany to visit her family before

Figure 3.3: Countess Elizabeth Wolff-Metternich – bequeathed a significant legacy to The Loreto College in Ballarat, allowing for the completion of the Chapel

making this commitment (Barry, 1975). Tragically, whilst nursing a sick child she died on the ship home. However, her legacy lives on in the chapel that her bequest brought to completion and that has been treasured by generations of Loreto girls, not only whilst at school but also for their weddings! (This bequest had arrived at Mary's Mount on the Feast Day of Elizabeth of Hungary.)

One of the highlights in my final year at Mary's Mount was the bus trip to Melbourne for the International Eucharist Conference of 1973 which was held at the MCG. There were 97,000 students and teachers who had bussed in, which was a massive gathering, larger than I had ever seen. We were proud to hold up our banner with the Loreto crest amongst all the other Catholic schools from Melbourne and other country areas. The top banner words of 'Maria Regina Angelorum' translate as 'Mary, Queen of the Angels'. The lower section, 'Cruci Dum Spiro Fido', means 'Whilst I breathe, I trust in the Cross', a link to the Ignatian tradition that Mary Ward so admired. We wore this on our blazer pockets as did every other Loreto school, both nationally and internationally.

Outside of school, some aspects of the Church were much slower to change, particularly in regard to other religions. I remember being a Girl Guide in the Presbyterian parish of St Cuthbert's when I was about 12 years old. I loved it and all went well until there was going to be a Church service. I was not allowed to go unless I got permission from our priest, and he was not keen. This was also a time when if you were marrying a non-Catholic you had to get married in the sacristy instead of the main church. Promises also had to be made by the non-Catholic partner to baptise children 'as Catholics' and send them to Catholic schools.

Overall, the years of my later primary and secondary years until I graduated from school in 1973 were times of experimentation in

Figure 3.4: Interior of Mary's Mount Chapel, Loreto Province Archives, Australia & South East Asia

the Church. Churches were built with innovative architecture and artwork and music evolved with more engaging, less pious hymns. On the other hand, the Australian Church had to deal with a great exodus of priests and religious brothers and nuns as society changed. The rules were more flexible but there was an increasing absence of young people in pews. Schools had increasing numbers of lay teachers on the staff rather than nuns or brothers. With the development of artificial contraception in the mid-1960s and the Church's ensuing encyclical, *Humanae Vitae* (1968), and its decisive stance against abortion, there was an exit from the Church of women and some men who could not accept this teaching. This resulted in a consequent weakening of the unconditional acceptance of papal authority that had existed up until this time. These themes will emerge more strongly in the next chapter when Ann and I consider our young adult years.

## References

Barry & Gilliland, B, *Loreto by the lake: Mary's Mount, 1875-1975*, 1975.

Buchanan, MT, 'Pedagogical Drift: The evolution of new approaches and paradigms in Religious Education', *Religious Education, 100* (1), 2005, pp. 20-37, retrieved from https://www.proquest.com/scholarly-journals/pedagogical-drift-evolution-new-approaches/docview/199330782/se-2?accountid=8194

Latinovic, Mannion G & Welle, OFM, *Catholicism Opening to the World and Other Confessions*, *Vatican II and its Impact*, 1st edition, 2018.

Loreto College Victoria, accessed February 18 2022 from https://loreto.vic.edu.au/loreto-college/heritage/philanthropy/countess-elizabeth-wolf-metternich-bequest-circle/.

## Reflection

1. What do you see as the positive features of each of the approaches, such as the *My Way to God* textbooks or the different types of retreats or reflection days for students at this time?
2. What structural changes have you noticed in modern churches compared with more traditional ones? What values underlie these changes?
3. Were you part of large Catholic gatherings like Bernadette describes?

# Part 2

# Specialist

The religious educator is also an authority in this model, an expert, a specialist who provides a properly documented and scientifically and morally solid background to the various life philosophies and religions. In this way s/he can also critically evaluate and/or deconstruct certain aspects of the religious/ideological traditions, both within and without Christianity (Pollefeyt, 2008, p. 9).

Figure 5.1: Christian Living Camp, 1976

## CHAPTER FIVE
## University Days and Early Teaching – Bernadette

*Two roads diverged in a wood, and I—*
*I took the one less traveled by,*
*And that has made all the difference*
(Robert Frost).

In 1974 at the age of 17 I headed off to Melbourne University to begin a Bachelor of Arts degree. I had been fortunate to get a government-funded Studentship which served to pay for my accommodation at St Mary's College and give me some much-needed pocket money. St Mary's College in Swanston Street adjacent to the university had been founded by the Loreto Sisters in 1918 and was the first Catholic university residential college for women in Australia. I was fortunate that I had the opportunity to stay here as otherwise university would have been very daunting for me, with no friends from my school and a very different environment from my school days. As it was, I made long-term friendships over my three years there, and had many fun times with the St Mary's community, and the community of the Newman College for boys next door which was run by the Jesuits. In my Dip Ed year, I moved into a shared house in Flemington with my friends from St Mary's: Cath, Maureen, and Rachael.

My experiences of Church over these years was diverse. I have memories of low-key masses in the small College chapel with Fr Bren Donohue which I loved, and occasional visits to the eclectic university church of St Carthage's in Parkville.

However, the most significant religious memories for me were times my friends and I spent with the St Mary's principal, Sr Elizabeth Nowotny IBVM, and two Jesuit scholastics, Stan Lim SJ and Chris Gleeson who later became a much loved principal of Xavier College, Kew. We would have reflective Christian Living camps away where we would discuss the 'big questions' of life all in the spirit of Vatican II. These discussions broadened my understanding of Church and started me on a more adult spiritual journey. Stan would also sometimes take us to visit the Jesuits' Corpus Christi Home for Men at Greenvale. This home for marginalised or alcoholic men had originally been opened up by Mother Teresa and her Missionaries of Charity, who had come to Melbourne in 1970 and set up a convent in Gore St, Fitzroy. They saw people living on the edge of society, just as in India, and in 1974 opened up Corpus Christi on a bush site at Greenvale to provide not only material support for the men, but friendship and a sense of dignity that many may never have experienced. In 1977, as the numbers swelled to 80 men, the Missionaries of Charity entrusted Corpus Christi to the Jesuits and the Mercy Order. Spending time at Corpus Christi also broadened my horizons and would lead to further outreach opportunities some five or six years later.

## First Appointments as an early career teacher

After completing my Bachelor of Arts and a Diploma of Education, I began my teaching career in 1978 at the tender age of 21. Like it or not, I needed to teach to fulfil my three-year teaching bond. My first appointment was to Hamilton High School. Hamilton was a regional town of approximately 10,000 people (at the time), about four-and-a-half hours drive from Melbourne, but only 3 hours from my parents in Ballarat thanks to the very direct route of the

Figure 5.2: All dressed up for *The Music Man*

Hamilton Highway. I had at this time purchased my first car, a little yellow Holden Gemini which tootled up and down that highway at least once a month. Beginning teaching at this time was jumping in the deep end, with no mentors or anything else in the way of support in dealing with demanding classes. I found to my dismay that the Year 11 and 12 Maths students were just three years younger than me. However, I made the most of my time in Hamilton, by taking advantage of its natural features, such as its proximity to the Grampians in one direction and Portland in another, playing lawn tennis, being a Girl Guide leader and being part of the chorus in local musicals. I had some fun times with these musicals, such as the *Pirates of Penzance* and *Brigadoon*, loving the companionship, dressing up for the parts, and the lovely music. I also at this time began to learn the flute from a visiting teacher, which was a joy.

After my three years in Hamilton were completed, I decided to make a move. Having read the novel, *All the Rivers Run,* which is set on the Murray River, I decided to move into the Catholic system and apply to St Joseph's College, Echuca, which is also located on the beautiful Murray River. In those days, a letter to a principal was all it took to get a position. I was still very much a country girl at heart during these days, having no thought of going back to Melbourne to teach. I soon got to know locals in Echuca by again playing lawn tennis and getting involved in musicals, such as *The Pajama Game* and *The Music Man*. St Joseph's was a Brigidine co-educational college of approximately 600 students. Having to teach Religious Education for the first time was a challenge, but I was very well supported by having two Brigidine sisters from Melbourne, Reba and Catherine, coming up to Echuca once a month to help me plan my lessons. They enjoyed the warmer climate of Echuca for the day and I got to prepare great lessons and learn more about the Brigidine tradition.

The Brigidine story is based around six young women who were drawn together in 1807 by Dr Daniel Delany, Bishop of

Kildare and Leighlin, Ireland, who helped them to form a religious community in Tullow, County Carlow. He named them the Brigidine Sisters, after St Brigid, the 5th century saint of Kildare. In 1883, the Brigidines were requested by the Bishop of Maitland diocese to come to Australia. Thus the first Brigidine convent was at Coonamble, NSW. The second major foundation was at Echuca, Victoria, with a new contingent of nuns coming from Tullow. The St Brigid's cross was adopted by the Brigidine order and is worn by all sisters on their lapel. The Brigidine spirit is one of 'engaging with the issues of our time, standing in solidarity with the oppressed and seeking to build a more inclusive community' (Brigidine Sisters). This was very evident in the St Joseph's community which embraced me with open arms and supported me as an early career teacher. I have memories of Sr Athanasius who worked with me at Year 7 level, teaching the students new hymns such as 'Glory and Praise to our God' and 'Lift up your hearts to the Lord'. The Religious Education (RE) Curriculum was what Buchanan (2005) would call a Life-centred approach. It focused on the teaching from Vatican II that stressed God was present in all things, with the sacred and secular world intertwined. The *Guidelines for Religious Education for students in the Archdiocese of Melbourne* formed the basis of lessons that were delivered. This process was structured around the following:

- Experience shared
- Reflection deepened
- Faith expressed as we come to know our Catholic faith
- Insights reinforced as we gain further insight and respond (Engebretson, 2002, p. 38)

These early days of the 1980s were also still a time of exploring new ways to express liturgy and new hymns were emerging all the time. These new ways included having liturgical dance at school masses, where mainly girls would dress in cream or purple flowing robes and perform ritual movements at certain points in the Mass. This practice was never fully encouraged by the Church and mostly does not occur today, but at the time it was a good way to engage young women in a male-dominated liturgy and add a colourful element to the Mass.

Whilst at Echuca, I began a Graduate Certificate in Religious Education at Aquinas College (now Australian Catholic University) in Ballarat, travelling there three or four times a term for intensive classes. This reflected the growing trend for adult formation in faith, with many more courses of study and seminars being offered in the 1980s and following (Campion, 1988). I was fascinated by the way the lecturers such as Sr Veronica Lawson RSM opened up scripture for me – her teaching planted a seed that would see me study considerably more scripture and theology in years to come. However, I was starting to find the constant travelling a burden, and so decided to move from Echuca after 2 years and return to Melbourne to teach in 1982 at Our Lady of the Sacred Heart School (OLSH) Bentleigh. Here I would also complete my Graduate Certificate of Religious Education at Christ College, Chadstone. The Daughters of Our Lady of the Sacred Heart were founded by Fr Jules Chevalier who was a Missionary of the Sacred Heart (MSC) in 1874 in Issoudun, France. He encouraged the sisters to 'embrace the risk of mission without limits' so as to spread a love of the Sacred Heart of Jesus throughout the world.

My three years at OLSH were a time of great discernment: at the end of 1985 I made the significant decision to return to the Loreto sisters and become a novice with them. The Novitiate was a period of two years of learning about the Order, new experiences, and reflection. I moved into a two-storied house in Corsewall Close in Hawthorn with Novice Mistress, Sr Ellen, dear old Sr Sylvester (who had taught me Modern History for a whilst at Mary's Mount), Sr Wendy, and Colleen (a second-year novice). My first year there was quite challenging in experiencing a very different lifestyle and completing a 30-day retreat at Pymble NSW with the Jesuit novices. However, my horizons were definitely broadened by spending time each week at Sacred Heart Mission in St Kilda. This was a venture by Fr Ernie Smith to feed the homeless in St Kilda each day. I would help prepare the meals and socialise with the visitors. In the afternoon I would sometimes accompany prostitutes or single mothers to medical appointments.

In my second year I was fortunate to be able to travel – by bus – from Victoria to Broome, Western Australia, to work at St Mary's school for three months. This was a school run by the Loreto sisters. I also got to visit the Loreto outpost of Lombadina Mission further north, and Turkey Creek and Derby. In those three remarkable months, I encountered the culture of the First People of Australia and learned a great deal. However, the latter part of my second year back in Melbourne was often restless and I became increasingly aware that although I still wanted to help people, I could do this just as well as a lay woman. I ended up leaving the Order the end of 1987 amid many tears and uncertainty as I was very fond of the numerous friends I had made within it. However, it was the right decision and I have never regretted it.

The following year, 1988, is one I have tried to forget as I was adapting to teaching again, this time at Kildara Brigidine College in Malvern. I was happy to be back with the Brigidines after my time in Echuca, but my early days at Kildara were difficult, mainly from a family perspective. My dad became seriously ill and died of cancer in May of that year, only a month after having been formally diagnosed. It was a complex time for the rest of that year, grieving for the loss of my dad whilst trying to support my mum in Ballarat, who was devastated by the sudden loss of her husband of over 30 years and at the tender age of 57. As well I was dealing with school issues and uncertain housing. However, the darkest night is often before dawn and the following year was just so much better: I moved to Collingwood into a shared house in notorious Easey St and met my husband, Paul, at St Joseph's parish.

St Joseph's parish was a wonderful parish run by Fr Michael Casey. There were many parishioners around my age or older who had been in various religious orders but left and gravitated here. The parish had a strong social justice focus, being involved in Catholics for Peace, social housing and supporting refugees. As well, there were social events such as Parish Weekends and drama groups, and it was in these groups that Paul and I met. Over the coming year or two, there were many engagements announced in the parish and the last of these was us.

At this stage, I had moved to Santa Maria College Northcote to teach, as Kildara College was beginning to close down. Santa Maria was established in 1904 by the Sisters of the Good Samaritan and it had a Benedictine charism. The Benedictine tradition dates back to the 6th century where St Benedict established a rule for his monks based on hospitality and caring. The Good Samaritan sisters were founded by Archbishop Polding in 1857 as an Australian order charged initially with caring for the poor, particularly abused women. Their mission was then broadened to include teaching in schools, with Santa Maria being founded in 1904. Its College motto was, 'Dare to do as much as you are able.' At the end of Term 1 at the school I was married at St Joseph's Collingwood and we moved into a Housing Co-op house that was part of the parish. This was a form of social housing whereby a government grant was attained to pay for the houses and then those who could afford to, like us, paid normal rent, whilst those who were struggling paid minimal rent. We would support each other with different housing projects, such as repainting a kitchen or setting up a garden. However, after a year or more we felt like buying our own home, so we moved out and rented for a whilst in North Fitzroy before buying an affordable house in Northcote. It is here that our two children were born – Damien in 1994, who sadly only lived for 22 hours because he was very ill, and our beautiful, healthy daughter, Erin, in 1996. Whilst I was still on maternity leave, in 1997 we sold our Northcote home and moved to Ivanhoe. I did not return to Santa Maria after my leave ended as part-time work was not on offer, but instead procured a part-time position as a Pastoral Associate at St Joseph's Church, Northcote. This drew on my past parish experiences, especially at St Joseph's, Collingwood, and involved working closely with the parish priest, Fr Michael O'Connell, to build up parish life, enhance liturgy and co-ordinate a joint school and parish sacramental program.

We made this our parish and made many friends over the five years I worked here, with Erin also going to primary school there. The Easter Triduum was a highlight of parish life with innovative ideas coming from Good Samaritan Sr Margaret Smith SGS, including communal washing of feet on Holy Thursday and everyone coming up to the large font to sprinkle water over themselves in the Easter Vigil. We also used to go to Palm Sunday rallies each year under the parish banner and do the Good Friday Stations of the Cross at All Nations Park in Northcote. The strong sense of social justice in both the Collingwood and Northcote parishes that we were involved with served to significantly shape my faith and political affiliations.

Inspired by the parents in the parish sacramental program, I decided to begin a Master of Theology by research with Sr Maryanne Confoy RSC – a Sister of Charity – at the United Faculty of Theology (UFT). The program involved both children from St Joseph's school and children from neighbouring state schools who wished to make their First Eucharist. After an initial introductory session, parents worked through an interactive booklet with their children over several weeks. I would visit them to support the parents and discuss how things were going. They then celebrated in small groups of about 4 or 5 families. I interviewed parents before and after their child's preparation and celebration and then drew on Fowler's Stages of Faith to analyse my findings. The ways the parents had grown in faith was significant – they really appreciated the process they had been through and seeing their child take their turn at reading or bringing up the gifts, which may not have happened if they were celebrating in a large group.

After five years I decided to move back to school and was offered a position as Religious Education Coordinator at Genazzano FCJ College. The story of these and the following years are in Chapter 7.

# References

Brigidine Sisters, retrieved from https://brigidine.org.au/about-us/our-beginnings

Engebretson, K, 'Writing church sponsored religious education textbooks' *British Journal of Religious Education,* 25, (2002), pp. 33-45.

Fowler, JW, *Stages in Faith: The Psychology of Human Development and the Quest for Meaning*, Harper & Row, New York, 1981.

# Reflection

1. What have been the formative influences in your own faith development?
2. What religious orders have you experienced or known about in your own education? What aspects of their works, lifestyle and/or charism appeals to you?
3. Life has its ups and downs, as you can see from this chapter. What have you learned from challenging experiences in your life? Have these experiences shaped your own religious development or drawn you away from religion?

## CHAPTER SIX
## University Days and Early Teaching – Ann

*What you are is God's gift to you, what you become is your gift to God.*
Hans Urs von Balthasar.

After school, I kept up with the FCJ Sisters, especially Sister Maryrose Dennehy who would become, for me, something of a guiding light until her death in 2018. I have her picture on my desk at work today as a reminder of all the goodness and grace she disseminated in her long years of teaching and her profound influence on generations of Gen (Genazzano) girls.

The nuns thought that I was a possible candidate for a vocation. Perhaps they recognised something in my adolescent yearnings, in my way of being in the world that had prompted them to think of me as a fit for the consecrated life. But I was eighteen and life held other meanings for me. It did not help that on that post-school retreat for the discernment of a possible vocation, Father Geoff James SJ delivered a letter to me from my then boyfriend. Temporal temptations and opportunities took hold and the appeal of a vocation was readily displaced by the urgencies of new friends, a new independence and the fun and games of the Law Revue at the University of Melbourne.

I had managed to get into Melbourne University because I had a language, Italian. I sang a robust version of 'You Don't Have to Say

You Love Me' in my badly accented Italian as my oral component to get across the line. I also worked hard to get a Special Distinction for English and my name is now fading on an honour board in a dim dark corridor, that brief celebrated moment of distinction. Law was a complete mystery to me, and it was a classic case of getting into that faculty because I had the marks. I knew a legal career was doomed when I failed the introductory subject, Legal Practice, bored as I was with legalistic minutiae and convoluted language. I managed, however, to pass Criminal Law and later completed a minor in criminology with the Bachelor of Arts majors in English and History.

My university career was average at best, although I starred as a fabulous K-Tel sister in a couple of Law Revues as Steve Vizard honed his skills, later doing a couple of shows and solos with the Tin Alley Players. I played C-Grade netball for the university for a season, and spent a lot of time having tea and biscuits in the John Medley building. Aah, those days when a good cup of tea and some Arnott's Monte Carlos did the trick. My handwritten essays were turgid in the extreme and I spent a lot of time lazing on the lawn outside the Baillieu Library as my medical student friends dutifully trooped off to lectures. Café Paradiso and Tiamo's were well patronised in those days of bad philosophy and bibulous discussions.

During this time, I shared a small bedsit with my sister in Hawthorn. My mother had moved us out when I was nineteen and my sister seventeen, because family life was probably just too chaotic with the other four children still at school and one at kindergarten. We did lots of odd jobs to pay the rent; cleaning, babysitting, clerical work, invigilating at school, some tutoring. It was a wonderful time with few responsibilities. My faith life continued, but my attendance at Mass was less regular. The one place I continued to visit was Saint Francis' in Melbourne CBD, that work-a-day church open to all, a homely sacred space in which to pause and pray and think and light candles for departed loved ones in the Ladye Chapel – something I

Figure 6.1: Sr Maryrose Dennehy fcJ

Figure 6.3: Ann (second from right) with Tin Alley Players

do to this day. I love seeing people in fervent prayer, some kneeling, some with rosary beads, a couple reverently touching a framed image of Our Lady.

I marvel at the candles with their ardent little flames flaring heavenward. Together with a couple of tapers, there are now (March 2023) the Health and Safety lighters available for use, something my Year 9 students did recently when we visited the Ladye Chapel on our Catholic Identity Immersion Day. One of the continuums of Catholicism is the sense of communal praying over time. The prayers I uttered as a teenager half a century ago may not be so different to the invocations my own students make today. I may pray just as a sixty-five-year-old woman prayed when the church was built in 1842, a mere seven years after the founding of Melbourne by John Batman. Those million candles lit each year at this welcoming church are a sign that the prayers of the faithful are as important as ever.

With my brand-new BA, I joined the Public Service and for five years worked for the Ministry of Housing. Here I interviewed prospective tenants, allocated emergency and waiting list accommodation, visited clients in Heidelberg and Broadmeadows, dealt with neighbourhood issues, tensions and rent arrears, and realised that my life was privileged and sheltered compared to many. I worked second jobs in bars to pay the rent in other accommodation and lived in Rathdowne Street, Carlton with two other sisters for a whilst, and then in a share house in Scotchmer Street, North Fitzroy. I hosted parties, laughed a lot, dreamt of a different life, was conscientious enough at work, caught up with Sister Maryrose when I could and had my heart broken. By then I had decided I had better do the overseas trip, as I was well behind my peers who had already been on the mandatory Contiki tour in their university holidays.

I left Melbourne in 1984 and returned permanently in

1992. During those eight years abroad I lived in London, in Bournemouth, in Cornwall, in Scotland, on the Channel island of Guernsey, and on the Isle of Man. I did all sorts of work; in bars, cleaning, chambermaiding, selling kitchens, singing in a resident band, picking daffodils, working in a theatre, cooking, hostessing in a restaurant, being the administrator for a small architectural firm, being Auntie Annie in a holiday camp, joining the pub trivia team to win our round on British TV, dancing under the glitter ball at a local disco, having a letter to the editor published in *The Times*. It was an extended holiday, even when there were bouts of hard work, and eventually I knew I had to come home. One thing I always did was to visit churches to light candles and pray. I always felt the pull of faith and the rituals that held me tight. So, approaching 35, I came home to sing at my best friend's wedding at Newman Chapel, fulfilling a promise I had made to her at sixteen when we were not paying attention in Mr Duncan's Year 10 Maths class.

Back in Melbourne, I worked for Telecom for nine months whilst I was doing a professional writing course and living with my sisters in Balwyn. I met my husband on this course, both of us aspiring writers, both needing real jobs. Like recalcitrant school kids, we would pass letters across the room to each other and he actually proposed to me this way.

My father was briefly disappointed when I married – to a Protestant. Because I wanted to have the blessing of the Church, my future husband, who was divorced with two children, sought an annulment of his first marriage so that I could enjoy the sacramental nature of our union. For those outside the Catholic Church, this is something hard to understand as an annulment has no legal standing. It does not invalidate the legitimacy of the children from the former union. The decree of nullity is a declaration by a specially convened Tribunal that at the time of the first wedding there was some essential element lacking between the couple for a valid marriage to take place. Essentially, the Church is making a retrospective judgement on the validity of the original bond and the intentions or capacity of one partner at the time of the vows. This means that the Church can interrogate and ask awkward and invasive personal questions about the previous marriage so as to ensure that there was a reason to invalidate it. In my case, my husband's former wife took umbrage (and this I can appreciate) that some wholly unrelated ecclesial body was making a ruling on her marriage. From what I understand, she was vehemently angry towards a member of the Tribunal as she responded to this process and it may well have added to the wounds she was already carrying.

I could not wait forever for the Church's decision on the annulment so we were married in a small country Presbyterian church by a pastor who had all the makings of a television evangelist. I wore a daffodil silk Laura Ashley dress and my flower girls carried sunflowers. Two and half years later, and with a three-month-old daughter, the annulment was approved, and we had a ratification ceremony at Our Holy Redeemer Church in Surrey Hills conducted by dear old Father John Brosnan, the man to whom Ronald Ryan gave his last confession. Father Brosnan was well loved, a priest of the old-school and a 'dyed-in-the wool' Geelong supporter. After Father Brosnan, Father Peter Priestley became our parish priest (PP), a thoughtful man who was also chaplain for the Airforce down at Avalon. It was he who had to make sense as he spoke to children at Mass and at school after the 9/11 bombings. There were tears in the pews when he told us one Sunday that he was leaving the priesthood. In his early fifties, he had found late love and the congregation wished him every blessing, aware that he would receive little or no support financially from the institution he had loved and served so faithfully. Meanwhilst, my husband and my father became good friends, spending many a Sunday afternoon robustly debating religious issues, with me presiding and intervening with placatory platitudes and cups of tea.

## First Appointments

So there I was, married and still needing a proper job. I completed a DipEd. at the University of Melbourne and got my first job on a part-time contract at my *alma mater* Genazzano in 1995. I had run into a former teacher and we got chatting and she told me to ring the principal with her recommendation. I did and I was in the door. This was a gentle start to my career as a teacher, and because I was familiar with the school story I felt very much at home. In my second year, I took three months off to give birth to and care for my daughter, and then I went back to work part-time, my dear husband bringing Grace down to my staff room for breastfeeding.

During this time, I began to understand more about Ignatian spirituality as I had a couple of senior RE classes and dutifully did the pre-reading to be one lesson in front of the girls. School-based workbooks and readings were collated and the notions of reflection, discernment and meditation were seen as just as important as the acquisition of religious knowledge. Student work was assessed through looking at journal entries and reflective writing, although there was a generosity in that, perhaps even more so when a student wanted to carefully critique a view or position held by the Church. This was a nod to the fact that students were about to leave school. The capacity to think critically and respond to the vagaries and vices outside the confines of the convent on Cotham Road, Kew, was a necessary tool in their armoury, spiritual and otherwise.

A growing realisation of the influence of Marie Madeleine d'Houët, the founder of the Faithful Companions of Jesus, became apparent as her story was now told with great enthusiasm by the school leadership and was embedded as an integral part of the evolving school story. Her key words about courage and confidence became something of a mantra for staff and students. Her lovely quote – *Let us make good use of our time on this earth. Let us do all the good we can, whilst we can* – can be seen as anticipating the later words of our own Australian saint, Mary of the Cross MacKillop who opined *Never see a need without doing something about it*. This wider knowledge of Marie Madeleine enabled me to look more deeply into the local FCJ initiative and appreciate the sacrifices made by the early sisters who sailed to the colony of Victoria at the request of the Jesuits. These mainly young women knew that they might never see their loved ones again. I was and am in utter admiration of their courage and conviction as they set out to educate what would become generations of Catholic children, all for the love of God. The FCJs, together with the Mercys and the Brigidines, the Loreto Sisters and the Sisters of Charity, amongst other orders such as the Jesuits, Marists, Christian and Lasallian Brothers, came over these years to educate in life and faith the children of the colony. In so doing they built the foundations for the strong Catholic education system in operation today. We are in their debt.

After my contract work at Genazzano finished, I found further contract work at Korowa Anglican Girls' School in Glen Iris teaching English, and just managing the basics in Unit 1 Psychology. (Teaching out of an area one has not trained in has always been a part of the versatile kitbag teachers carry.) After that, I spent a semester at St.Bede's in Mentone, a Lasallian school based on the charism of Saint John Baptist de la Salle, a French educational leader and innovator who cared that the poor had an education in life and faith. A Lasallian education prioritises faith in the presence of God, quality education, inclusive community, concern for the poor and respect for all persons. I learned very quickly that being short in a room of growing Year 9 boys did nothing for my management skills. And I was not about to assume a military demeanour to get a small paragraph out of them as we studied John Marsden's *Tomorrow When the War Began*. So, on occasion, I resorted to the old trick of an early release to lunchtime and cricket on the oval if the work was completed. Brother Phil helped me out a lot when the boys rioted and Brother Quentin was a beautiful calm presence as he walked through the school and had a word for everyone. The boys were good-natured, but they bounced basketballs on walls and kicked the desks of the boy in front of them just for a laugh – all that energy confined to a classroom and a female teacher who cared about words, whilst they cared about wickets.

I was teaching Year 9 RE all about human relationships, respect and dignity, and the boy-girl relationship, and the boys found this both embarrassing and an opportunity for all sorts of comments and asides with which to amuse their mates. I spent a lot of those lessons blushing furiously. The boys joshed each other a lot and one dear lad, Terry S, was ribbed mercilessly because one day in his eagerness to tell a story he inadvertently called out 'Mum' to get my attention instead of Mrs Rennie. My six months at St Bede's confirmed that I was better suited to teaching girls, especially after those days when I would come home and cry from frustration, exhaustion and the dread of the next day. I truly thank God that I had the earlier experience at Genazzano which had shown me I could do a good job in a conducive climate. I toughened up a bit after St Bede's and have since come to admire those female teachers who can handle boys, and their openness and energy. During this period I had completed a GradDip in RE as I saw my future teaching as staying within the Catholic sector.

After this, I started my Masters in Religious Education and attended lectures on Tuesdays and Thursday nights at Christ College (ACU) in Chadstone. Somehow, this study gave me a bit of ballast as I enjoyed learning and doing the assignments. And I was very impressed with Dr Kath Engebretsen whose teaching style, knowledge and evident enthusiasm for her subject really worked for me. I was fortunate to have lecturers who were able to convey their understanding clearly and I benefited from their insight and wisdom. One of the good things about the Masters course was that although there were certain subjects that were mandatory, there was also some choice. I was pleased to do a unit on women monastics and mystics in the Middle Ages, looking at Hildegard of Bingen, Mechtild de Magdeburg and the Beguines. Fruitful study helped me during this challenging time. Today I can look back and see my six months in Mentone as a time when I began to ascertain where my skills and interests lay and how I could best use these for myself and for others.

As I reflect on this early outing in my teaching career, it makes me realise how crucial those first few teaching placements are for the inexperienced teacher. I was reasonably confident but my spirit was crushed, albeit briefly. One wonders about those who may have been gifted teachers, but whose experience was so destabilising that they decided to leave the profession altogether. I have known wonderful teachers who have given it away after a couple of years. I have also known wonderful teachers who have taught for twenty years or more, those who have assessed at VCE level and whose students have won Premier's Awards, and who have found that they cannot keep teaching because they have been so demoralised and diminished by their later classroom experience. And I know many committed and faith-filled teachers who have steadfastly remained in the system, despite professional setbacks and classroom shenanigans and the occasional feeling of being overlooked and undervalued because they bring their hearts to school. It is these teachers, and especially those just starting out, whom we must look after if our Catholic education system is to thrive in the future.

This is even more so the case for the teacher of Religious Education today, especially so in a classroom that may be neutral, resistant or antagonistic in an increasingly secular pluralist world that is almost post-Christian. In our Catholic schools we will always have our confessed pupils, some of whom are churchgoing, many of whom may be baptised but do not know much about the faith because it no longer carries the primacy or authority of times gone by. The common understanding and connections made in the days of our Catholic childhood are not apparent today and we are working in some classrooms that have little catechetical background. Catholic primary schools do a wonderful job, but the reality is our secondary classrooms are a mixed bag of faith dispositions and inclinations.

As has been said before, the Catholic school is the Church of the future and our students often arrive as pretty blank slates. The job of the RE teacher is to bring our young people to a faith that is active in loving God and loving neighbour; to evangelise in a way that brings the gospel alive and makes it relevant for today. Bernadette and I will consider this issue in a later chapter and make some suggestions as to what can be done to ensure a reciprocal flourishing for both student and teacher. At the heart of the Religious Education conundrum is the question as to whether we are educating in a particular discipline or witnessing our faith tradition. The answer is in finding the balance between the two that serves our students well as they negotiate their way in a constantly changing world. Religious Education must reflect the reality of the times if it is to carry some weight in the spiritual and holistic formation of the next generation.

My early teaching career had me travelling far and wide across Melbourne, and because I do not drive I had plenty of time on public transport to think, plan and prepare for lessons. Or read for pleasure. For two years I caught the 6.53 am train from Surrey Hills station to Belgrave, almost an hour's journey to the distant Dandenongs. On alighting next to Puffing Billy I would puff up the hill to Mater Christi College, a Good Samaritan school. I was fortunate to work under Sister Margaret Keane SGS, a wonderful school principal whose faith was vibrant and who had the ability to see the big picture as well as the small detail. Here, I was introduced to the VCE subject Texts and Traditions by Kevin Whitehouse, a mentor who took a great deal of time to prepare me for the classes we ran concurrently on the timetable. This was a new subject for me with its exegetical approach and its theme-based interrogation of the Gospel of Luke. As well as teaching this subject, I was introduced to the Benedictine charism and St Benedict's Rule, the same order Bernadette worked with at Santa Maria, Northcote.

Archbishop John Bede Polding, an English cleric from Downside Abbey, founded the congregation – The Sisters of the Good Samaritan of the Order of St Benedict – in the colony of New South Wales in 1857. The Good 'Sams' were to go out into the world where the life chances for many were limited through ill-health, poverty or other circumstances. They engaged in missionary activity with single mothers, the destitute, alcoholics, former prisoners trying to go straight, the Indigenous, the illiterate children and the many marginalised who needed a listening ear, a compassionate heart and practical help to improve their situation. Over the course of his lifetime, Archbishop Polding came to understand the Australian 'tyranny of distance' and to appreciate its different Catholic/Christian sensibility as compared to that experienced in Europe.

For one of my assignments for the Masters in Religious Education I was still undertaking, I interviewed Sister Maureen Keating SGS about her religious life and its meaning for her. She obliged me with her honesty and warmth about the life she had chosen as a young woman. She spoke of the importance of Benedictine spirituality as the primary impulse for all other activities and looked back at her vocation with joy for what she was able to do for others. At Mater Christi, a number of the staff were imbued with the charism of the Good Samaritan Sisters and I

## University Days and Early Teaching – Ann

remember how beautiful some of the reflections made by staff were. Often these staff were not RE teachers, but Maths or Technology teachers who could find God in their own discipline and lend him to the rest of us for those special moments in a staff meeting. There was a lovely climate of collegiality at Mater Christi and I felt I was, at last, coming into my own as a teacher at about the five-year mark. During this period, for professional learning I also started doing VCE English marking with VCAA at the end of the year. This became something I did for almost fifteen years. Around this time I also began contributing the odd article on faith, education and the joys and travails of the classroom, to various media outlets.

I was sad to leave Mater Christi, but I had applied for a job closer to home and had prayed to get it. I was thrilled when I was notified that I was to take up a permanent position at Siena College in Camberwell, a short hop on the 612 bus or a brisk forty minute walk, with a stop in Maling Road for a coffee on the way. During my time at Siena, I taught Texts and Traditions, English, and English Literature at VCE level as well as English and RE at other levels. I was a House Coordinator and Year Level Coordinator. In my first year one of my students received a Premier's Award for Texts and Traditions and I began to feel as though my repertoire of skills was coming to fruition in this more academic study. As well as this, I was inducted into the charism of St Dominic and we staff enjoyed warm homilies from Father Anthony Fisher (now Archbishop of Sydney) and Father Martin Wallace who had spent many years doing missionary work in the Solomon Islands. As a middle school leader, I was invited to attend conferences and retreats that involved the nourishing of the soul and the deepening of the Dominican story.

Of particular interest and enjoyment was the pilgrimage a number of staff made to Fanjeaux in France where St Dominic stayed a decade in his attempt to convert the heretic Cathars. We visited his birthplace in Caleruega in Spain and steeped ourselves in his fascinating story and the founding of the Order of Preachers in 1219. We were also able to interrogate the four pillars on which the Dominican charism is built: community, ministry (service), study and prayer. A knowledge of these founding characteristics enabled me to understand the sort of education offered in a Dominican school. Today, Siena has a short break for whole school prayer/stillness/silence in the middle of the timetabled school day as it honours its abiding commitment to this reflective, gentle and transformative practice.

As an RE teacher, I highly recommend the importance of such pilgrimages in coming to an understanding of a founding charism. My experience suggests that this builds a new connection with the story which can be more expressively realised in the classroom. The teacher can then speak out of authenticity and something of an insider's knowledge which in turn translates into witness of that charism and the generative passing on of the original story, but refreshed naturally for the time and place of contemporary telling.

After seven good years at Siena, a Religious Education Coordinator (REC) position was advertised at Genazzano and I applied, and was successful in obtaining the position. This was about coming home and I was thrilled to be back at the school that had nurtured me. Dear Sister Maryrose was living in the convent next door and regularly popped into various staff rooms for a chat. Staff were appreciative of her gentle wisdom and her genuine interest in their family lives. Having been school captain and a former principal, she knew everyone associated with Genazzano and their brothers at Xavier and their cousins from the country. At her eulogy it was noted that she was the LinkedIn of her time! With Maryrose and the other FCJ sisters a visible, although reduced, presence, the students still understood the connection to the greater story. There was much amusement in the school when a couple of sweet junior girls thought that Sister Maryrose was Marie Madeleine. I know I joked with her and said she was my own personal saint and she would shush me and laugh.

During this time, I was also completing a Masters in Educational Leadership at ACU. This involved some weekend units undertaken in Ballarat, so whilst I listened to lectures my husband and daughter visited Sovereign Hill and would be ready to meet me as soon as class was over. Again, I really enjoyed this Master's study and was particularly pleased that in one of my units, under Brother John McMahon fms, I was enabled to explore Australian religious poetry, looking at landscape and character, history and hubris, as part of an appreciation of the spiritual sensibility that this land of the big red heart and its ancient narratives could evoke. This research was later published in *Champagnat*, the Marist journal.

As REC my job was to work on curriculum to ensure we covered mandated work appropriately, enlivening it with the FCJ story and its lived charism, and giving licence to the teacher's expertise in delivering this well and building the faith community. There had been much formalising of the RE curriculum over the years since my first foray at Genazzano in 1995, so by the time I became the REC in 2008, new approaches were embedded and the study of our own faith tradition had taken on a relevant, sequential and student-centred approach. There was a growing appreciation that this special subject had a complementarity of direction with both the cognitive and affective domains being impacted. RE was essentially part of the Catholic student's faith formation in the class, but it was also a subject to be taken seriously and taught as rigorously as any other on the school timetable. It was engaging the head, the heart and the hands – that holy trinity of thinking, feeling and doing. This was especially apparent in the various missionary causes for Vinnies or Caritas or the FCJ Sisters that had girls inventing multitudinous ways to fundraise. Learning and doing as evidenced in the Ignatian notion of *contemplatives in action* was the impulse for outreach. Loving God and loving neighbour were as important as ever!

## Reflection

1. First appointments are crucial in a teaching career. They can make or break and it is well known that many young people leave the profession before the 5-year mark. Reflect on your own experience and those people, events, interactions and structures which supported or challenged you at this time.
2. Have you seen teachers struggling? In what way?
3. How have you overcome dispiriting or challenging aspects in your teaching career? What strategies have you found helpful in regaining optimism and /or agency?
4. Have you been able to discern the similarities and differences in congregational charisms?

# Part 3

# Moderator

But at the same time the religious educator is also a moderator. S/he realises that her/his confessionally constitutive identity is not the only meaningful correlation that can be developed from human experience and that human experience itself is a multi-interpretable reality. S/he accepts and confirms that also other valuable representations exist of the human search for meaning in life. And s/he is ready to moderate and steer students along the process of complex and multifaceted correlations that they develop between their own experiences and religious and non-religious traditions (Pollefeyt, 2008, p. 10).

# CHAPTER SEVEN
## Changing Landscape

*We have a big job ahead of us as we fulfil our mission educating those one in five children in Australia who attend our systemic schools.*
(NCEC, 2017)

Between us we have acquired multiple degrees and clocked up more than 50 years in Catholic education, with some of that time in leadership roles as Religious Education Coordinators. How curious it is that we have both been RECs at Genazzano! Over this time, we have seen different approaches and strategies ebb and flow and the composition of our classes and teams of teachers diverge and differentiate. As Michael Buchanan (2005) highlights, there has been 'pedagogical drift' in Religious Education, with Church authorities and education commissions trying to respond to changing circumstances in society in the light of Church teaching:

> When viewing the development of each approach in relation to each other, there emerges a 'drift effect,' where aspects of the pedagogical techniques and the rationale associated with a particular approach surface in a distinct yet related paradigm. This phenomenon is referred to as "pedagogical drift (p. 20).

Our earliest teaching experiences in the 1980s and 1990s

were with the life-centred approach of the Guidelines of the then CEOM (Catholic Education Office, Melbourne). However, over time it became obvious that although this approach was good in a relational context, it did not equip students with the skills to critically understand their faith and consequently there was a large gap in student knowledge (Rymarz & Engebretson, 2005). In the late 1990s, an educational approach emerged that placed emphasis on the formal, cognitive study of religion. This had two major implications for Victorian Catholic schools.

The first outcome was that two Victorian Certificate of Education (VCE) courses were developed for senior students: Texts and Traditions Units 1- 4 which emerged out of the previous units of Biblical Studies, and the new Religion and Society Units 1-4. Texts and Traditions can be taken by students from schools with different faith backgrounds, but in a Catholic school focuses on biblical texts, ranging from the Hebrew scriptures in Units 1 and 2 to Luke or John's gospel in Units 3 and 4. Religion and Society can also be taught in a wide variety of contexts. This subject considered issues of religion and identity, roles and rituals in different religions, how believers experience religion, and challenges to religions and religious adherence (Engebretson, 2009).

Unit 2 specifically considered ethical issues. Here, teachers were given a considerable degree of choice in this course, being able to choose the religion/s they focused on and the particular challenges and ethical issues they considered. This permission meant that a teacher's expertise or specialist interest was invested in the curriculum delivery. Unit 3 considered defining features of religion in terms of nine aspects such as texts, rituals and social structures, whilst Unit 4 analysed challenges to the Church, both historical and contemporary, and how the Church responded.

Both VCE courses have endured for more than 20 years as students and teachers generally seem to like them. Teachers have acknowledged that students learn well in these units at a senior level, especially if the content aligns with the students' abilities to interrogate historical material, analyse, write fluently, and critically appreciate biblical context. A solid faith background provides some contextual advantage in studying Texts and Traditions, although the subject could be undertaken simply as an academic exercise. Whilst different chapters and themes are studied each year, Text and Traditions offers an array of different ways into learning about New Testament times, the message and ministry of Jesus of Nazareth, the gospel as a literary text and the exegetical process. We are pleased to say that both of us had Genazzano students receive Premier's Awards for Texts and Traditions, Bernadette in 2003 and Ann in 2008. These were students who worked hard, asked questions, showed deep and engaging interest, and wrote many practice essays. So this recognition was thoroughly deserved. (As an English teacher, Ann just wished her students knew the difference between *it's* and *its*.)

This increased flexibility enabled new growth and relevance for different school settings. For example, in keeping in touch with the immediacy of the students' lives, a film could be used as a vehicle for opening up an ethical issue. Topical issues headlined in the local, national or global news could also be explored in a proactive and responsive way, encouraging student participation and discussion. Here, the teacher needed to be mindful of the Catholic teaching or position on some issues and the changing and challenging secular response. The ability to mediate and moderate judiciously in a classroom where enquiry and contest is encouraged is part of the intellectually invigorating nature of this subject and certainly one where the students have much to contribute.

The second outcome for the Educational approach was the introduction of the *To Know, Worship and Love* (TKWL) textbooks that were implemented in all Catholic schools in 2001 and 2002 for students from Prep to Year 10 in the Archdiocese of Melbourne. These texts were written by the Catholic Education Office staff under the leadership of the Vicar for Religious Education and aimed to emphasise, 'the acquisition of knowledge, as a vehicle for spiritual and personal faith development through attending to knowledge, understanding and critical inquiry' (Engebretson et al., 2002, p. 19).

Despite teachers initially distrusting these textbooks, fearing they would be too conservative and not liking to be told too definitively what to teach, the implementation continued (Rymarz & Engebretson, 2005). The texts covered Church history, beliefs, rituals, sacraments and moral education. The use of these texts encouraged teachers to use formal assessment and report on this for the first time which, in turn, often enhanced the status of Religious Education in schools. Moreover, the texts seemed to help teachers who had limited background and they also encouraged some teachers to gain more background knowledge by undertaking academic study (Rymarz & Engebretson, 2005).

Bernadette:

*To Know, Worship and Love* (TKWL) was used during my two years at Genazzano and my early times at Xavier College, Kew. It was mandatory for students to have a copy of the textbook, so it was put on their booklists. As a Religious Education Coordinator (REC), I encouraged teachers to not solely use the textbooks but to supplement them with videos and collaborative activities. Because of the more cognitive focus of the textbooks, teachers were encouraged to give tests and, at Xavier, there were midyear and end-of-year examinations on the content. For Ann also, Genazzano, too, had students buy the book and this was used as the basis for many units. However, within the curriculum study there was licence to incorporate other teaching resources to add depth and detail. *To Know Worship and Love* was useful in that it set out its ideas concretely, was written in accessible language and understood that reams of text was not going to assist in the student learning process. The inclusion of artworks, graphics, graphs, photographs and other visual stimuli was useful. Of particular note was the way that anecdotes and lived experience were used as the opening to many topics. Links were made that were relevant to the lives and age/stage of the students. With the advent of the digital version, the textbooks ceased. Today, students in most Catholic schools have access to the digital version of *To Know, Worship and Love* and this continues to be a beneficial resource.

The digital version of *To Know, Worship and Love* is much more interactive with puzzles and games, YouTube clips, maps and audio and other sensory stimulation. However, the language is unambiguous. There has been a recognition that the contemporary student has different learning needs and inputs and that time and resources are key to student engagement. Thankfully, we have moved away from the one-size-fits-all pedagogical paradigm of the past.

For example, neuroscience is now being used to interrogate how the brain works and what processes make for better learning outcomes for the individual student. What has emerged across a number of disciplines is the debate as to quality and whether the rigour of the past has been short-changed by today's digital colour and movement. The digital arcade has its attractions, but there must be a tempered use of these resources as we continue to honour the modes of reflection, immersive reading and deep thinking that have brought us thus far. The use of drama, improvisation and play are other effective avenues for exploring RE topics, as is time given to personal journaling which is often a conduit to other intuiting. The best resource, however, is of course the quality RE teacher.

Ann:

With the changing demographic of the Catholic school classroom and the changing pedagogical landscape, this is a more invitational approach where the tone in TKWL, though certainly confessional, is not heavy-handed. *Australian Catholics* magazine has adapted magnificently to the times under the leadership of Michael McVeigh, with a teacher hub active with the latest resources, articles and podcasts, and a youth orientation that makes the material engaging and relevant. Teacher professionalisation via Zoom webinars is also offered. Genazzano was the first school in Australia to have four students undertake the Young Journalist immersion programme to produce the annual Spring edition of the magazine.

Today one of the appeals of this print/digital magazine are the articles, commentaries, interviews, graphics, song and film lists compiled by student writers, as well as the more considered articles from Andrew Hamilton SJ and the humorous letters to saints by Michael McGirr. Garratt Publishing also has online resources written by Dr. Gavin Brown to complement their wide range of Catholic publications that support and professionalise the RE teacher. *Understanding Faith* is another excellent resource with its multimedia activities, archival footage, recent statistics, glossaries and language tailored to age and stage. Of course, RE teachers are resourceful and can mine all forms of media for the latest material that resonates with youth culture. Of particular note and great use is the MACS REsource website which is frequently updated and user friendly and provides up-to-the-minute liturgical material.

For senior classes, *Eureka Street* provides thoughtful and topical commentary with a range of contributors who canvas the concerns of the day and often use the Catholic lens to interrogate them. The writing is routinely good, so I sometimes manage a sneaky English lesson in there as well! These differing resources can be accessible entry points for the unpacking of ideas and issues as this acknowledges the diversity of students in the contemporary classroom and the immediacy of certain modes to engage their attention. For the RE teacher, the morning ping of CathNews into the inbox daily is a must. This aggregates Catholic news across Australia and the globe and is a great way of having a broad handle on what is happening in the Church. Understandably, RE teachers will have their own resources and many schools subscribe to *The Tablet, America* or the *National Catholic Reporter*, as well as reputable international or local liturgical sites and particular congregational websites which enhance the global reach and message of various religious orders.

If there is a criticism about digital resources, it is one applicable to all subjects in this age of laptop learning. A student can easily flick between screens and other work/site/media can be visited when they should be focusing on RE. My personal experience more recently has been to catch students out playing Tetris and doing work for other subjects or looking online at clothes. It is just a quick tap on the shoulder to get them back on task, but I do feel like a 'Roaming Catholic' when I have to walk around the class to check. This laptop dependency has accelerated over the course of the Covid 19 pandemic and is an issue that has spring up now that students are back to face-to-face learning. The catch-up for learning gaps occasioned by almost two years of home learning is apparent, as is the need to reinvigorate the discipline needed in accessing technology at appropriate times.

The other more recent phenomenon that is reverberating throughout the education system globally is the fact that many students no longer read the way we did. The tomes and texts of the past do not engage, the movie version is easier to digest and much youth literature is about issues and an immediacy reflected in their lives and experiences. Language shifts, interculturality and the democratisation of the internet, as well as diminution in attention, means that educational pedagogy and content has to be remodelled to align with the times and the students we have in front of us.

The 21st century has unveiled vast paradigmatic cultural and social change. The consequence of this is a declining receptivity to Christianity and its relevance as a moral framework. As such, teachers in Catholic schools will have noticed a discernible change in attitude towards the study of RE. However, in spite of the secularity of the times, in faith-based schools we prioritise Religious Education on the curriculum. It is a stand-alone subject and provides time for more than just facts about faith. As ever, there is always the acknowledgement that the parent is the first educator of the child and that what we do grows on that. However, in our time-poor world and with loosening ties to parish life, it would appear that learning about faith has been outsourced to the Catholic school. This is in line with what is happening elsewhere in the curriculum where many life skills are now undertaken at school, effectively replacing parental input and oversight. All sorts of wellbeing education now comes under the school's parameter as the timetable is diversified to meet needs.

However, RE still retains its special status and there is the hope of formation, too, although we may never know where those seeds we plant bloom. That fine balance between the sacred and secular, the cognitive and affective, prayer and pedagogy, needs to be negotiated by the teacher who knows what works in their classroom. As Rossiter (2017) notes, 'the healthy Catholic school RE program needs to retain a creative tension between ecclesiastical concerns and the teacher's views about the spiritual/moral needs of the pupils' (p.16). Today, we are more aware of the interdependence of the mental, emotional and spiritual aspects that promote student wellbeing and how the realisation of life satisfaction, meaning or purpose is twinned with a personal manifestation of spirituality unique to each individual.

As Bernadette notes, one of the things that has been done increasingly to engage and diversify the curriculum is visiting places of religious worship or story, both Catholic and other. This has invited a new understanding and insight, openings to fruitful dialogue that build respect, tolerance and understanding. In responding to the richness of other traditions and the questions, answers and worldviews they are immersed in, the Catholic student can expand and clarify their understanding and connection to their home tradition. This is building towards the common good for all, one of those outcomes that cannot be assessed, except by the God who sees all. The grace of a faith response is always hoped for in the RE classroom, but it is ever an open and invitational setting where there is no coercion, only inclusion. The social justice imperative that has become a significant part of the enacted RE curriculum has enabled students to experience what it is to reach out to others in need. Here, they can come to a real understanding of Jesus' message of justice and inclusion and can learn that they have the agency to change lives.

Of note is the Friday Night School program that both Xavier and Genazzano participate in each week. Students spend an hour or more with students from the nearby Richmond Housing Commission flats – helping with homework or explaining concepts and ideas. Until recently, at the end of each year Xavier hosted a residential weekend for disabled children to enable some respite for parents. This has just been changed due to Working With Children restrictions and other compliance issues, but it is hoped that a daytime alternative will continue. It has been gratifying to see the number of young men and women who have just finished their VCE exams volunteer to assist here. (To be fair, this is often before Schoolies!) They are truly exemplifying what Pedro Arrupe, former Superior General of the Society of Jesus, called *men and women for others*, a term he coined in 1973 for those who follow the Ignatian way.

Students at Genazzano engage in the 'Companionship' programme from Year 5 onwards. This is an outward looking programme that honours the idea of accompaniment of others so the youngsters may visit a local nursing home to bring some

Figure 7.1: Australian Catholic University, Melbourne campus

brightness and chatter to the elderly. This notion of companionship is at the heart of an FCJ education as it opens young hearts to the experiences of others in the hope that empathy and compassion are enacted. These immersions can be truly formative and shape what may be the actions and attitude of later life.

Retreat days are taken at Amberley, Templestowe or Lysterfield, places which have monastic histories and today are being repurposed for the next generation and their faith development. Immersion days have students head to the city to visit St Patrick's Cathedral, St Francis' in Lonsdale Street, the Mary MacKillop Centre and the recently opened Mary Glowrey Exhibition at the Australian Catholic University. Via the local parish, some students have made the trip to (the back of) Bourke in New South Wales for an Ignatian Immersion and work with the local indigenous community. Both Genazzano and Xavier offer a three-week Kimberley scholarship to four students to raise awareness of the Indigenous story here and to bring back ideas and insights to share with the wider school community.

Students also visit temples, mosques, shrines and synagogues to hear about the other faiths and their rituals, beliefs, structures, symbols and community rules that make us such a multi-faith country. The students learn that we share much in common with other faith traditions and this breaks down ignorance and opens up dialogue. They visit places in the city such as the Big Issue office and other outreach initiatives to see the reality of lives on the streets, to open their eyes to their own privileges and good fortune, and to sow the seeds of possible future philanthropy, in whatever way that may come to fruition.

Bernadette:

As Ann has indicated in earlier chapters, Genazzano has a strong focus on the life of Marie Madeleine d' Houët. At Xavier, the focus is on Ignatius of Loyola. The story of Ignatius is of a young Spanish man of noble birth who became a knight. He was hit by a cannonball at Pamplona in 1521, sustaining a serious injury to his leg. During his convalescence, Ignatius read two different types of books. The first type were stories about the life of Christ and the saints. The second type were normal secular novels. Ignatius found that when he read the first type of stories he felt happy and excited and wanted to read more, whilst when he read other secular stories there was no such reaction. He was to call the first feeling *consolation*. The opposite kind of feeling of unrest and confusion was named *desolation*. These two feelings became part of a process known as *discernment*.

After recovering from his injuries, Ignatius went on to free himself of all wealth at Montserrat, made a pilgrimage to Rome and then spent a year at Manresa, where he begged for his food and spent extended periods in prayer (*Who was Ignatius Loyola*, 2022). What Ignatius was feeling is summed up in the famous prayer he wrote:

> Take, Lord, receive all my liberty,
> my memory, my understanding, my whole will,
> all that I have and all that I possess.
> You gave it all to me, Lord; I give it all back to you.
> Do with it as you will, according to your good pleasure.
> Give me your love and your grace; for with this I have
>     all that I need.

Ignatius' experiences at Manresa led to him writing the Spiritual Exercises that are still being used almost 500 years later in two forms: The Full Spiritual Exercises are offered over a 30-day period and the book titled *The First Spiritual Exercises*, containing a program which is followed over four weeks in daily life (Hansen, 2013). Ignatius went on to attend the University of Paris where he met Peter Faber, Francis Xavier and others whom he convinced to join him in forming 'Friends of the Lord' – later to become the Society of Jesus.

My time at Xavier over 13 years gave me many opportunities to experience Ignatian Spirituality through retreats and professional learning. I liked the focus on finding God in all things and the simple but powerful ways of experiencing the Spiritual Exercises when opportunities arose. In classes, Year 9 students learnt in detail about Francis Xavier, after whom the school was named. Year 10 focused on Ignatius in the context of their unit on Changing Church and the Protestant Reformation. Most classrooms had the initials AMDG inscribed on the whiteboard - the Latin words *Ad maiorem Dei gloriam* meaning 'For the greater glory of God'. This is the motto of the Society of Jesus.

A prayer that students would say from memory before each RE class was the Prayer of St Ignatius:

> Dearest Lord,
> teach me to be generous;
> teach me to serve You as You deserve;
> to give and not to count the cost,
> to fight and not to heed the wounds,
> to toil and not to seek for rest,
> to labour and not to ask for reward
> save that of knowing I am doing Your Will.

As the Religious Education leader, I was responsible for the Year 9 and 10 classes at the Senior Campus. The *To Know Worship and Love* curriculum was enriched by excursions for Year 9 to St Patrick's Cathedral, St Francis' Church and the Mary MacKillop Centre, whilst Year 10 visited Buddhist and Hindu temples and Jewish synagogues as part of their study of World Religions. The latter

Figure 7.2: Year 10 Xavier students at a Jewish synagogue in Elsternwick.

activities would have been seen as heretical in the pre-Vatican II world of our earlier chapters but were very valuable for students in an increasingly hermeneutical context, allowing them wider comparisons for analysing the scriptures that we were studying, as we shall see in the next chapter. Another activity for 10 volunteers from Year 10 was called Building Bridges. Students would gather after school at different campuses on five or six occasions during Terms 2 and 3. They would be shown around the participating schools such as Bialik Jewish College and Preston Islamic School then join in small group discussions led by student leaders. The gatherings would conclude with a vegetarian meal. These were wonderful occasions for broadening student horizons and breaking down stereotypes.

It was during my time at Xavier that I decided to become involved with Teachers Across Borders. This was a program that involved both Australian and USA teachers volunteering their time in Cambodia over a 10 day period during the January and June holidays to provide professional development for teachers. I was fortunate to be able to visit Battembang in 2007 and Kampong Thom in 2009, teaching Maths to the Cambodian teachers with the help of a translator. These experiences broadened my horizons greatly and gave me much enjoyment and life.

## References

Belmonte, A and Rymarz, R, *Leading Catholic Schools: A Practical Guide for Emerging Leaders*, Garratt Publishing, Melbourne, 2021.

Buchanan, M. (2005), 'Pedagogical drift: the evolution of new approaches and paradigms in religious education', *Religious Education*, 100:1, 2005, pp. 20-37. DOI: 10.1080/00344080590904662

Engebretson K, 'Writing church-sponsored religious education textbooks', *British Journal of Religious Education 25*(1), 2002, pp: 33-45.

Engebretson K, 'Phenomenology and religious education theory', *International Handbook of the Religious, Moral and Spiritual Dimensions in Education. International Handbooks of Religion and Education, vol 1*, edited by de Souza et al, Springer, Dordrecht, 2009, https://doi-org.ezproxy2.acu.edu.au/10.1007/1-4020-5246-4_46

Hansen, M, *The First Spiritual Exercises*, Ave Maria Press, 2013.

National Catholic Education Commission: A Framework for Formation for Mission in Catholic Education, 2017. (Foreword: Archbishop Timothy Costelloe.)

Rossiter, G, 'Postmodernity, faith and recontextualisation: An agenda for religious educators', *Journal of Religious Education*, 2013, pp. 68-72.

Rossiter, G, 'A personal critical perspective on the development of Australian Catholics Schools' Religious education: Where to from here?' in A. Belmonte and R. Rymarz, *Religious Education in Australian Catholic Schools: Exploring the Landscape*' Garratt Publishing, 2017.

Rymarz, R and Engebretson, K, 'Putting textbooks to work: empowering religious education teachers', *British Journal of Religious Education*, *27* (1), 2005, pp. 53-63, https://doi.org/10.1080/0141620052000276528

Xavier University, *Who was St Ignatius Loyola?*, 2002 [online] Available at: https://www.xavier.edu/mission-identity/xaviers-mission/who-was-st-ignatius-loyola [accessed 3 March 2022].

## Reflection

1. What changes or 'drift' have you noticed in the delivery and reception (teaching and learning) of Religious Education in the past few years?
2. Has there been a discernible change since the pandemic?
3. What resources do current students respond to or engage with most readily?
4. Where do you find 'entry-points' to engage with students?
5. Have you accessed or explored the congregational website of your school? Have you been able to engage in person with the charism through discussion and discernment with a professed member of this religious order?
6. What in-house programmes encourage social justice initiatives amongst the students?
7. How do your students meet and dialogue with students of other faith backgrounds?

# CHAPTER EIGHT
## Today's Context and its Implications

*In an environment in which, for many reasons, students from a range of faith backgrounds other than Christianity find themselves in Catholic schools, the multi-faith aspect of religious education can no longer be ignored*
(Rymarz & Hyde, 2013, p. 36).

## A social landscape of change

The environment in which Religious Education is taught in Catholic schools in Australia today has changed dramatically from the experiences we described in earlier chapters. Culturally, this reflects the significant changes in society globally and, in particular, the impact of religious affiliation in Australia. Due to successive waves of migration from Europe, Asia and Africa, Australian society has become much more culturally diverse. Our own Catholic faith has been blessed with its multicultural strands. Participation in religions such as Hinduism, Sikhism, Islam, Judaism and Buddhism continue to grow each time a census is taken. Even more significantly, we live now in a 'post-Christian and post-secular context': post-Christian in that Christianity is no longer the accepted worldview of the majority of people, and post-secular in that even presuppositions about secularity no longer apply (Boeve, 2016, p. 41).

By this Boeve (2016) means that people are tending to move from Christianity to a more nuanced position – rather than a more extreme opposite of atheism or secularism. Here, they choose to experience the divine in personal situations such as meditation and turn to the Church only for key life events such as marriages and funerals. In addition, 39 per cent of Australians now identify themselves as 'No religion' (2021 Census, ABS) – the first time in Australian history that this has overtaken the number of Catholics (*Sydney Morning Herald*, 28 June, 2022). And, whilst Christianity, and in particular Catholicism, remains the most common religion in Australia according to the 2021 census, Christianity has dramatically fallen from being 88 per cent of the Australian population in 1966 to 44 per cent, whilst Catholics form now only 20 per cent of the population (2021 Census, ABS).

In terms of Mass attendance, where once it would have been considered a mortal sin not to attend Mass on a Sunday, according to more recent national counts of attendance, 'only about 11.8 per cent of Australia's Catholic population, or 623,400 people, went to church on a typical week' (National Centre for Pastoral Research, 2021, p. 1). Of these 623,400 people, it is interesting to note that the median age is 59.3 years, whilst the percentage of those attending Mass in the 15-24 age group is 6.9 per cent. In reality, most Mass attenders are between 60 and 74 years, and the number of grey heads continues to grow. (Need we say, this, too, is our demographic.)

## Implications for Catholic schools

The implications for schools are obvious. Whilst the numbers of students attending Catholic schools has grown at a steady rate as seen in Table 8.1, the religious composition of school communities has changed significantly.

Just over half (58.2 per cent) of Catholic primary and Catholic secondary students (56.3 per cent) are nominally Catholic, whilst

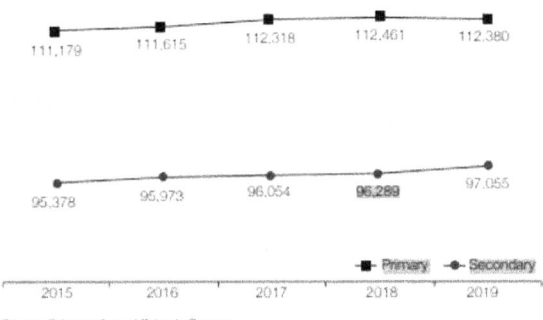

Table 8.1: Student enrolments in Catholic Schools in Vic (CECV, 2019) over five years.

just under half (48.1 per cent) of Catholic primary and similarly of Catholic secondary students (43.7 per cent) attend either a government secondary school or a private (not Catholic) school (ABS, 2016). Attending a school other than a Catholic school would have been unheard of in the 1960s era in which Ann and I grew up, with non-Catholic partners having to promise to send all their children to Catholic schools before they could be married in a Catholic Church, according to Canon Law. With big families and discounts for successive children, the Catholic schools of the 1950s to the middle 1970s were at their peak affiliation, with a large proportion of religious sisters and brothers taking on the teaching load.

These statistics are played out in diverse Australian classrooms that might include Indigenous students, families where one or both parents were born overseas and students from other Christian – such as Orthodox – traditions and other world religions. However, Chambers (2012) suggests that far from considering this diversity a problem, it is an asset, 'for it is the Catholic school's privilege that religious diversity is a characteristic of its clientele' (p. 192). Beyond religious diversity are other broader challenges facing Catholic schools in a world context which is variously described as 'post-Christian' and increasingly secular and individualist (Boeve, 2012).

Communal attitudes of shock, anger and shame at a Church that covered up pedophilia in the past decades (as revealed by the Royal Commission) have stripped the institution of much of its moral authority. Clericalism, hierarchical intransigence and the lack of a female voice within the Church have accelerated disillusion and disappointment amongst the laity. Aligned with this, Sheridan (2018) asserts that popular culture is overtly hostile to Christianity and 'because Christianity is so associated with Western civilisation, Christianity is cast as a primary villain in the world today (p. 20).' In our Catholic schools, we have a multitude of worldviews, a few of which may be negative towards Christianity, some indifferent, others nominally supportive and others cultural or confessional. This is the reality of the contemporary classroom in the Catholic school; the classroom where religious education is undertaken as part of the school's mission and identity.

Ann:

What is becoming increasingly apparent in today's society is that the story of Jesus of Nazareth and the claims of Christianity are no longer common knowledge or an entry point to understanding. The stories with which we were so familiar are becoming distant or sidelined by other attractions. Some have said that Christianity is now in exile. We only have to look at the ongoing debate over whether or not the Lord's Prayer should be recited at the opening of Parliament, as some consider it is no longer widely representative of the national constituency. Fifty years ago, these stories provided the building blocks of understanding and connection and the ultimate identity and cohesion of the worshipping community.

Today, the greatest story ever told is just one narrative in a competing and sometimes confusing mix. Boeve (2016) speaks of the accelerated erosion of the overlap between Christianity and culture as practically complete. The framework of faith that was so central to Catholic life when we were growing up has been marginalised. Our student cohort may be confessed, neutral, resistant or hostile; they may enjoy another faith tradition or they may have no tradition or an indifferent inclination to any transcendent belief system. However, the Catholic school has a place for them all. At the same time, the Catholic school becomes the place and ecclesial face of the Catholic Church in the 21st Century.

Catholic schools are schools for all. With that invitation comes the reality that our students will have various faith experiences and backgrounds, and that a one-size-fits-all pedagogy of the 1950s and 1960s is no longer appropriate or enriching for the learning experience or the spiritual growth of the individual. The Catholic students of those years, such as the two of us, had a uniformity of worldview, did not question the moral authority of the Church, and enjoyed the family and community cohesion of the tribe. We were catechised. We mixed with other Catholics, knew our prayers and feast days, and shared common understandings that made connections with each other easy. We did not dare miss Mass or Holy Days of Obligation and the rosary was recited with regularity.

The inputs and experiences we had were relatively innocent. We were not seduced by the smorgasbord of distractions that consume today's teenager. Technology was the family phone in the hallway and the small black and white TV on the back porch. Things were done *en famille* and any sort of privacy was a luxury, as most big families had two or three children sharing the same bedroom, on bunks usually! Children did not have rights or opinions, and education was delivered without differentiation or much acknowledgement of learning needs, cultural background or family situation. My four sisters and I wrestled with the same curriculum, delivered in the same way over almost twenty years. It worked for me, but two of them later felt short-changed by an education that did not recognise their individuality and their particular gifts and aspirations.

Today's students have an education system that recognises the individual in the learning equation much more readily and responsively. The days of rote learning and recitation are over, although there is still a place for memory work to do with timetables, periodic tables and the ability to read in a way that is measured and meaningful. There has been much pedagogical work done in education to put the student at the centre of their learning. Over the years we have had growth mindsets, flipped the classroom and used thinking hats, preferred learning styles, blended learning, backward design, positive psychology and any number of fads and phases – some useful, some simply modish. As we progress, we are still endeavouring to make each child's education fit who they are so they see themselves as competent, confident and capable of making a useful contribution in whatever sphere their talents and efforts take them.

We understand that the growth of personal agency is one of the positive outcomes of education, as is an increasing realisation of the soft skills of interpersonal transactions – especially in a world where technology can mitigate the face-to-face encounters needed for good socialisation and communal cohesion. What we have today is a growing continuum of tolerance for various beliefs and practices. Differentiation is now the key to many scenarios. Personal agency and initiative from the individual is accepted and often expected. Rather than being passive recipients of knowledge, the student is now in the centre of their own learning world.

However, the situation regarding religious education and the passing on of the faith tradition has changed unrecognisably. Greg Sheridan notes that Christianity is almost in existential crisis in the West and, 'Australia is about to become, if it has not already become, a majority atheist nation' (Sheridan, 2018, p. 2). Gerard Windsor contends that, 'The progress of the West from general belief to general unbelief has been inexorable' (Windsor, 2017, p. 228). Willian Sultmann in his doctoral paper (Sultmann, 2011, p. 1) refers to Diarmuid O'Murchu (1995) who has suggested that some of the social changes that are happening today are in the order of the agrarian and industrial revolutions, such is their scale and impact. As long ago as 1993, Marcellin Flynn in researching the culture of Catholic schools from 1972–1993 noted the influence of the secular materialist culture of Australian society as impacting on student interest in Religious Education, with a prescient parent response being that 'religious education in schools is, at best, fighting a rearguard action' (Flynn, 1993, p. 246).

Imagine then, thirty years on, the layers of complexity, disaffiliation and competing worldviews that are now apparent in the average Catholic school classroom. We are reminded starkly of Pope Francis' observation that we live in not only an era of change, but a change of era.

The increasing secularisation and a lack of familiarity with the Christian narrative and worldview, combined with classrooms that may have a number of students who are not Catholic and not interested, continues to challenge the teacher. We live in an age where social media shapes young minds and attitudes, the moral authority wielded by institutions in the past has declined and there has been a vital loss of the transcendent referent. The homogeneity of fifty years ago, which almost guaranteed a uniformity of response and a sense of identity and belonging, no longer exists. Cultural shifts have endowed people with new agency and voice as hegemonies are dismantled. This is a good thing, but it poses big questions as to how we continue to make RE rich and relevant for the next generation when religion has moved from the public to the private domain. As Windsor (2017) notes, 'Religion is off the radar as a matter for serious public discussion, which is a diminishment of the gravity and maturity of Australia's cultural life' (p. 231). How we manage the Religious Education in our classrooms today has multiple outcomes; some seen, many unseen in the formation of a mature and connected Australian society bristling with the promise of a shared future.

As Rossiter (2013) noted almost a decade ago, the challenge for the RE teacher today is that many of the children do not have a familiarisation with Catholic beliefs emanating from their own homes. We speak often of the parents as first educators in faith, but the reality is that this is true in only a small percentage of cases. The religious socialisation of the past has been greatly diminished by increasing secularisation. New patterns of socialisation are emerging in the digital age where new tribes and affiliations and niche groups are the current homes for identity and belonging. Cultural shifts have now prioritised personal ascendancy over the communal contract. Sharkey (2019,

p. 129) notes that the pluralising, detraditionalising and individualising cultural context is now taken as normal and normative by the majority of people. As such, the school is now the place for evangelisation of the next generation of Catholics. We have a big job ahead of us as we fulfil our mission of educating those one in five children in Australia who attend our systemic schools (NCEC, 2017).

This is the challenge for Catholic school leadership. Such leadership needs to prioritise and honour the nature and purpose of the RE classroom as the school maintains its *raison dêtre*. If it is on the timetable, co-equal and co-existent, with Maths and English and Science, why is it that this subject is the one that is routinely categorised as the one where students can miss class for other co-curricular activities, or where teachers are randomly pulled from RE classes mid-year to teach other subjects in need? Why is RE the 'poor relation' of the curriculum offerings in a Catholic school? It needs a revitalised respect. The question for us is how do we maintain the centrality of RE in a Catholic school whilst we compete for numbers and results in a marketplace that commodifies almost everything? How do we maintain the integrity of the subject at senior secondary levels when the students see it as an intrusion in the timetable, rather than an opportunity for reflection, increased religious and life knowledge, discussion and some necessary soul-building? How do we strengthen our distinctive Catholic identity in a world where schools can suffer from a diminution of vision and mission when this is not enacted routinely by those in the school community as a part of the daily fabric of school life? How do we assist the RE teachers who have 25 or more students in these core classes, whilst their peers have smaller class sizes and more overt investment in their subject because students feel these relate more directly to academic achievement and future pathways?

Our responsibility and privilege in the Catholic classroom is to nurture the human being in front of us, welcoming them and fostering in them the knowledge and growth that gives their unique and precious life meaning. Ideally, that is done within the Catholic context as host tradition, but we no longer indoctrinate or believe that other Christian denominations have a less-guaranteed way to God. Thank God, those divisive partisan days are over and we Christians, of different stripes, are so much more collegial in our faith. Ecumenism has opened many doors to understanding. We know that much enrichment can come from learning about other faith traditions, recognising in them other paths to the transcendent and the common care for others. Beyond the Christian belief system, we also know that we have much to learn and appreciate in the multicultural, multifaith world that is Australia today.

We also know that there is a great invitation for us to become conversant with Indigenous spirituality which honours Country as mother as we immerse ourselves in stories of ancient Dreaming. This openness to dialogue and understanding is practical and pragmatic in shaping the future egalitarianism and inclusion that will build a thriving sense of national identity and social cohesion. The Uluru Statement from the Heart offers a way forward as we look to the First Nations people as original custodians who can share the secrets of stewardship and kinship across this wide brown land we all call home.

Sheridan (2018) takes a cautionary stand when he reminds his readers that although parents may well claim a Christian identity, most of 'their kids will slough off by young adulthood' (p. 4). He refers to an increasingly nominal attachment to Christianity and argues that the family, not the school, is the most important factor in sustaining religious belief in young people. As teachers, we are in a front line position to see exactly what comes from the home via faith knowledge and practice. We can see the confessed and the cultural Catholic who return to the gospel values as foundational to the growth of character and its implications for the common good. We also invite enrolments from those who want the values and standards offered by a good education offered in a school which is faith-based.

There is a general acknowledgement that Catholic primary schools are good with discipline and standards and offer a warm sense of inclusion. They get the building blocks right for later development in this sector or others. At both primary and secondary levels, Catholic schools offer hospitality and the opportunity for evangelisation, as well as an openness to dialogue reflecting the context of the times. The expectation is that students who enrol in the Catholic school understand and accept that Religious Education and their participation in this curriculum and the school's liturgical celebrations is a given, even if they have no religious inclination or adherence elsewhere. There is an expectation that respectful reciprocity will be the attitude of those other students (and staff) who attend a Catholic school.

Our recent secondary experience suggests that there is a general if mild interest in matters of religious education from most students. Where there is great agreement is that the students all see themselves as spiritual beings who have their own ways of making meaning. This spirituality is personalised and idiosyncratic and picks and mixes from a variety of sources – traditional, new age, emerging and other. Some have called this the supermarket approach, where the student takes what they want and rejects those ideas or practices that do not fit in with their lifestyle or aspirations. It would seem that religion is seen as institutional and occasionally oppressive, whilst spirituality is very much a personal confection of ideas, attitudes and practices. There is a movement away from all sorts of traditional structures as new configurations and blendings take root and the past is viewed with suspicion and/or irrelevance. I have recently detected small clusters of disregard and, dare I say it, some subtle derision from older students about the faith narrative we hold dear. This may well reflect what is being said in the media and a general disparagement of the religious impulse, in particular Catholicism, in the light of recent events.

This is something that is being seen more frequently in

society, perhaps as a result of secularisation, with an increasingly contemptuous and critical assessment of Western Christendom and its legacy. Certainly there have been historical and structural sins, oversights, ignorance, paternalism and privilege and these need to be acknowledged and understood.

That being said, there are many people who recognise how important the Christian framework of morality and justice has been to our legal system and to many of the cultural, intellectual and social flourishings that have enriched the human experience across the globe. With so much activism – and some well-intentioned – at work geo-politically and with mood swings orchestrated by 24/7 social media, we must be mindful of finding that equilibrium that can bring about the common good. We must be truth-tellers in our own spheres, whilst acknowledging that the institution has been severely damaged and its former influence dissipated.

We have our challenges ahead and one of those is to ensure that our students have the capacity to think for themselves and not be swayed by the loudest voice. Nor do we want them to seduced by the virality of social media, the issue *de jour*, or the fear of having a dissenting opinion. We need to renegotiate a way to open up the Good News for them so that its universal story of love and redemption becomes meaningful for the reality of their lives.

There is an age and stage response to the impetus for faith as children mature. Many Catholic educators would be familiar with James Fowler's work and his *Stages of Faith* (1981) development theory that has been referred to in previous chapters. This has been called a psycho-theology based as it is on cognitive development. It is also based on an understanding that faith is not static across the life span. Naturally, our students begin to question, using their critical and rational capacities to examine what seems incomprehensible or wrong-headed in their estimation. They are leaving behind their *Synthetic-conventional faith* (Stage 3) understanding to transition towards a *Individuative-reflective faith* (Stage 4). They often reject or suspect the norms and paradigms that have come before, now moving towards new meaning-making that responds to growth, change, peer and wider influence, as well as the necessary individuation that takes place as old ideas are forsaken or critiqued and new ones tried. The Catholic classroom then becomes a place where robust discussion can be exercised. This, of course, will be well moderated by the competence of the RE teacher.

## Enhancing Catholic School Identity Project

One of the recent initiatives undertaken by the Catholic Education Commission Victoria (CECV) in partnership with KU Leuven University, Belgium, the oldest Catholic university in the world, has been the establishment of an ongoing project known as the Enhancing Catholic School Identity Project (ECSIP). The aim of this project is to understand, promote and deepen the Catholic nature of schools in Melbourne in the light of detraditionalisation and secularisation and what Gowdie (2017) calls 'ecclesial fracture' (p. 5).

This initiative, although more localised and targeted, is the result of a not dissimilar response to *the signs of the times* that heralded Vatican II. This significant phrase was used in two pre-Vatican documents *Humanae Salutis* (1961) and *Pacem In Terris* (1963), and four Vatican documents (*Unitatis Redintegratio* (1964), *Dignitatus Humanae (*1965*), Presbyterorum Ordinis (*1965*)*, and *Gaudium et Spes* (1965). It encapsulates the context in which these reforming documents evolved. *Gaudium et Spes* clearly articulated the state of the world almost 60 years ago in the following introductory statement:

> Today, the human race is involved in a new stage of history. Profound and rapid changes are spreading by degrees around the whole world. Triggered by the intelligence and creative

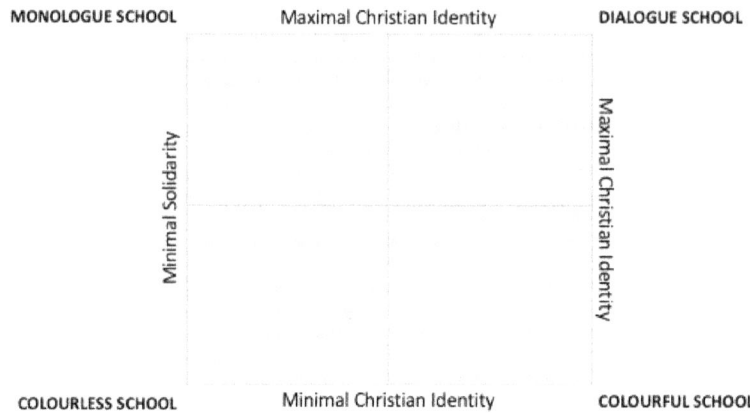

Diagram 8.2: The ECSI diagram of the four different types of Catholic Schools.

energies of man, these changes recoil upon him, upon his decisions and desires, both individual and collective, and upon his manner of thinking and acting with respect to things and to people. Hence we can already speak of a true cultural and social transformation, one which has repercussions on man's religious life as well (*Gaudium et Spes*, p. 4).

This statement is as true today as it was when first drafted in 1965. Individual and collective changes are impacting dramatically on the social, religious and cultural institutions that have bought society thus far. Carl Jung, writing a couple of years before Vatican II, referred to the importance of Christianity being seen in a new light 'in accordance with the changes wrought by the contemporary spirit. Otherwise it stands apart from the times and has no effect on man's wholeness' (Mackay, 2016, p. 49).

This was the zeitgeist of those times and now we are witnessing a phalanx of urgent signs for today. The Church and the world are evolving and we need to respond authentically, creatively and strategically to the challenges posed. Locally, we need to be constantly aware of the changing demographics of our Catholic schools and the worldviews that complement, critique or compete with Catholic tradition, doctrine and practice. We also need to acknowledge the severity of disruption caused by the pandemic and its impact on the norms and data that may have been expected under normal circumstances.

ECSIP aims to look to the future of Catholic education. It provokes serious questions as to the purpose and influence of the Catholic school and its religious identity. ECSIP also looks at navigating this responsively into the future. It proposes a hermeneutic-communicative understanding of education and a theological framework and vocabulary aimed at better understanding and clarifying Catholic identity as lived out in a school community.

This model proposes conversation with others about such matters as the confirmation, challenges and confrontations about one's own faith position that may ensue. Fruitful dialogue with the *other* is not seen as a threat, but an opportunity. ECSIP works with individual schools to interrogate their own internal landscape and to see how its population sees itself and what this says about its collective identity, daily practice and the degree to which its Catholicism is celebrated, or how it is diluted and diminishing.

The once-sacred has become increasingly secular. Or perhaps we should say that within the secular we need to look more closely for the sacred and sacramental. Our task is to find the path that will enliven what it means to be a child of God, a loving neighbour, a person of worth and dignity, in a life lived with purpose and harnessed to the common good of all. This is not simply a generic Christian values framework, but a vision and mission that is explicitly Christ-centred and Catholic. Rymarz and Sharkey (2019) warn against a generic spirituality and note that religion is a particularised experience and cannot be reduced to a community value or practice. ECSIP formally aims to identify the actual Catholicity of the school community. Its findings provide data that can be used to implement enhancement and discernment activities, amongst a range of interventions, to strengthen that identity.

As such, ECSIP is a tool used to evaluate the environment of the school and its daily lived reality (factual level), and compare this evaluation with what an *ideal school* (empirical normative level) might look like. It follows cross-sectional cohorts over periods of time to discern changes in the professed Catholic identity of a school. It is a practical response to measuring the pluralisation paradigm that is the context of the multifaith, multicultural educational environment in Australia today. In fact, Boeve (2016) considers this the most important of the paradigms and that it "shifts the place of Christian faith in the contemporary religious field" (p.

34). These surveys are completed by student, teacher, parent and board/governance cohorts so that a wide picture of the school and its religious influence is accessed. The diagnostic tools used are the Post-Critical Belief Scale, the Melbourne Scale, the Victoria Scale, the Profile Questionnaire and the Doyle Questionnaire.

The Post-Critical Belief Scale delves into an understanding of the attitudes towards religious belief and uses four categories of thinking to discriminate here; post-critical belief (symbolic affirmation), literal belief (literal affirmation), external critique (literal disaffirmation) and relativism (awareness of contingency/ openness). The Melbourne Scale, a dual-level measurement comparing current practice and the *ideal* school, aims to chart the measure of school identity in a pluralising context. It provides four types of school identity or perceived institutional operative modes. These are Reconfessionalisation, Christian Values Education, Secularisation and Recontextualisation. For the purpose of enhancing the Catholic identity of the school, Recontextualisation is the preferred option. The Victoria Scale explores how Catholic schools see themselves pedagogically. The Profile Questionnaire collects background variables to determine personal religious profiles, whilst the Doyle Questionnaire aims to collect data on the particular religious profile of the school.

These instruments are aligned with theoretical structures developed at Leuven and undergo continuous measures of scientific validation. Attitudinal or perception questions and statements are put forward and respondents' answers range from 'strongly agree' to 'strongly disagree'. Respondents contend with questions and statements such as:

*Is your school Catholic in name only?*
*It is easy to ignore my school's Catholic identity.*
*What is your attitude to the Catholic faith?*
*What is your personal religion or philosophy of life?*
*How often do you pray to God individually?*

*My school is a good place to grow closer to God.*
*In my school, people listen to the leadership of the Catholic church: the bishops and the Pope.*

## The KU Leuven Enhancing Catholic School Identity (ECSI) Project

With the aggregation of these responses, as well as current practice in the school, the changing landscape of the Catholic school can be ascertained. This comes down to the particularities of each school. The gap between real and ideal is where discussion and discovery happen. Respondents can choose to have their own personal ECSIP results graphed with explanatory definitions of the scales, together with their Doyle profile questionnaire.

With this knowledge, appropriate interventions or redirections can be made to ensure that the Catholic nature of the school is prioritised and is used to bring out the best in each student, regardless of faith affiliation or lack of such. Thus, there is a need for rich pedagogies that engage the whole person in both a humanising and evangelising approach that encourages dialogue, respect for *the other* and, as Paul Sharkey notes, 'aims at enhancing and enriching each student's awareness of their belonging and identity whilst at the same time sensitising them to the presence of those who make meaning differently' (Rymarz & Sharkey, 2019, p. 145). Here, a renewed Catholic identity engages with a multiplicity of views and voices and has those rich conversations which lead to reflection, discernment, tolerance and new understanding. With Recontextualisation, there is an intentional orientation which aims for the common good of all students. This necessitates the holistic formation and spiritual wellbeing and agency of the students.

Our aim is to reach and teach all students who attend Catholic schools. This is our task – this is our mission. As of May 2022, the Catholic education system nationally comprises 1755 schools, over 785,000 students and over 102,000 teachers across the country (NCEC media release 18/5/2022). According to Jill Gowdie, (Gowdie, 2017, p. 4) in 2016 only 19 per cent of teachers in Catholic schools in Australia were practising Catholics. That was before the Covid pandemic and consequent teacher attrition, especially from older teachers, who are often the backbone of the RE teaching programme in a school. This is a telling statistic if we want to enhance our Catholic school identity. Sheridan (2018) argues that the institutional Church needs to exercise situational awareness as a matter of urgency in the Australian educational context so that it can pass on the faith with a degree of confidence, aware that affiliation is diminishing, but there are still opportunities for new growth in less traditional ways. He suggests that Christianity must become a **bold** minority.

He also writes, and this is crucial in the context of the ECSIP, that Catholic schools are suffering from a crisis of faith. This is because there is a dearth of knowledge of the faith tradition such that our students' young minds rarely turn in the direction of the religious aspect of their lives. Rossiter (2014, p. 71) refers to the theology of interruption and recontextualisation as proposed by Lieven Boeve that underpins the ECSIP project. This is a theology that recognises the need for an enhanced quest for new understanding and interpretations for this age and a continual critique of the narratives we tell. This is especially the case for our students who are unfamiliar with traditional understandings and are increasingly religiously illiterate. Boeve suggests that a new contextual credibility needs to be a part of the theological discourse we present to our pupils (Boeve, 2016). We also need to address the language we use with our young people to ensure that it is not too 'churchy', alienating or obscure. Naturally, we need to treasure our liturgy and literature, but if we are to ask our young to keep the faith in ways that are authentic to themselves in this day and age, a new and revised lexicon is needed.

Both Bernadette and I can attest to the reality of the students' lack of familiarity with their own religious narrative. A number of my (Ann's) Year 9 students undertaking the ECSIP survey recently (April 2022) knew they were Catholics, but could not immediately make the link to the Roman rite. Of interest also is the fact that a number of students said to me later that the male/female paradigm for identification was limiting and the non-binary option should have been provided. Another sign of the times!

The ECSIP offers, via the data from the Victoria Scale, four evaluations of the identity and practice of a school that calls itself Catholic, as shown in Figure 8.2. This scale explores the pedagogical, moral and organisational choices of the Catholic school and its internal solidarity. These evaluations are:

> A monologue school = institutionalised reconfessionalisation/by Catholics for Catholics.

> A colourful school = Christian values education /active pluralism.

> A colourless school = institutionalised secularisation/neutral pluralism.

> A dialogue school = recontextualisation/living in the middle of plurality.

> The upper quadrants of the diagram indicate maximal expression of Christian identity, whilst the lower quadrant shows the minimal. The left and right quadrants respectively show minimal and maximal solidarity, with the term 'solidarity' indicating that there is a sense of collective cohesion within the school community.

## Today's Context and its Implications

These broad descriptors indicated in Figure 8.2 help us to understand the lived reality of each particular Catholic school.

Robyn Horner (2020) in her recent conference paper on the ECSIP writes:

> Three of the four responses we could make to the crisis of identity in Catholic schools – in which I mean responses to the fact that not only students and families, but also increasing numbers of staff question their identities in relation to the Church – actively lead to Catholic schools becoming more secular, not less (p. 7).

What is clear is that for Catholic schools the approach that most harmonises their *raison dêtre* with the reality of the world as it is today, is the approach of the Dialogue School. A Dialogue School retains its Catholic identity in a conscious and visible way. This is done whilst engaging in dialogue with other faiths, with philosophical and meaning-making systems in a world characterised by pluralisation, individualisation and detraditionalisation. A Dialogue School is a school where maximal Catholic identity and maximal solidarity intersect. It is a contemporary faith-based school in the midst of cultural and religious plurality, and it is a school that understands that such authentic dialogue can be a form of enrichment and appreciation. A Dialogue School has the capacity to reflect and renew itself, retranslating the faith for today and interpreting it through Post-Critical Belief. It affirms the way Catholicism can live vibrantly within a school and responds to the culture in which the school finds itself. A Dialogue School looks to the holistic identity formation of all who attend it, maintaining and preferring its Catholic identity whilst also being hospitable to the diversity encountered around it. As such, it offers *a theologically legitimate and culturally plausible discourse* (Melbourne Scale Video, 2013) between Christianity/Catholicism and the prevailing culture.

In its annual report for 2019, CEM (Catholic Education Melbourne), now known as MACS (Melbourne Archdiocese Catholic Schools), states that in that year 131 Catholic primary and secondary schools across Victoria participated in the ECSIP survey round, with 91 of these being Melbourne schools. All 131 schools received the new *ECSI Standard Report* inclusive of 'data-over-time'. This data-over-time is instrumental in illustrating the strength of Catholic identity between two quadrennial survey rounds, with the most recent being 2015 and 2019. This report indicates that schools have become more dialogical in their approaches to RE compared with eight years ago and that there is a stronger presence of Catholic identity. MACS hopes to build on these trends to accelerate this shift and to promote the future of Catholic education in Melbourne (CEM Website). However, that optimistic outlook has been challenged by more recent findings.

The MACS survey for the School Improvement Framework also asks questions as to the vitality, visibility and frequency of the Catholic religious dimension exercised in sector schools. This is drilled down to four capabilities; religious leadership, praying and celebrating, witness for mission, and learning. These capabilities look to the school's religious leadership in the *witness, specialist and moderator* model in its integration of faith, life and culture; the acknowledgement, assent to and celebration of prayer and liturgy; the public expression and witness of Catholic identity; and learning that reveals a dialogical, relational and optimistic pedagogy. Evidence of these capabilities being exercised in the school community, and to what extent, is gauged by student, staff and parent responses.

Recent data (2022) suggests that the Covid 19 pandemic interruption to onsite learning, and the application of usual school structures, protocols, formalities and familiarities, has had a marked impact on the Catholic Identity Domain. There has been a noticeable decline in the perceived effectiveness of Religious Education since 2021. This may be the result of two years of interrupted/home/digital learning and a 2022 spent navigating and remediating these deficits in our adolescent cohort that include learning gaps, the loss of social norms and appropriate behaviours, and the mental health tsunami that afflicts them. The lowest response rates from students related to how RE and Catholic beliefs addressed the reality of their lives (Years 7–12), their capacity to express views comfortably in the classroom, and the need for discussion of life questions and ideas. Positives noted were the primacy of prayer in the classroom, the celebration of sacraments and Mass, and the importance of social justice initiatives.

The staff response indicated a decline in school leadership discussion of mission and the sharing of leadership faith perspectives. Prayer was a prominent feature of all community gatherings, as was respect for the primacy of Catholic beliefs in sector schools. This data points to the crucial importance of school leadership, not just the principal, in affirming, aligning and integrating the mission of the school purposefully and repeatedly so that it becomes an organic part of the day-to-day lived experience of the community. Mission drift needs to be addressed urgently. In a world of disruption and uncertainty, clarity of purpose in our educational and pastoral endeavour needs to be seen and exercised by all who are engaged in this project.

Interestingly, just prior to the end of the 2022 year, MACS put out a survey to all Melbourne RE staff, those at the 'coalface', and invited them to forward this survey onto other subject teachers and stakeholders in the school to ascertain their (anonymous) perceptions as to how the RE programme was viewed at their school. The questions on this curriculum review were open-ended and there was room for the respondent to write as much or as little as they liked. Questions such as the following were posed.

What do you believe is the purpose of the Catholic school?

What do you think *makes* a Catholic school?

What do you see as the strengths/weaknesses of Religious Education in your school?

How is the content of Religious Education decided at your school?

Do you feel you know and understand as much as you need to of the Catholic tradition and culture?

Can you identify any actions we can take to build the confidence of teachers and leaders?

Do you believe the resources provided for RE are adequate for understanding where the Church comes from and what we stand for as a faith community?

The responses from this survey are expected to be illuminating, challenging and hopeful as 'honest to God' RE teachers tell it like it is in their classrooms. It would appear that the uncertainties of the past three years, and the frequent and undiluted amplification of this to our young people, have resulted in a decline in the sense of connection with Catholic identity. Action is needed to turn this around as we recreate the contextual credibility that underpins a viable and engaging curriculum.

## Today's classroom

Increasingly, religious educators are referencing the world in which the teenager lives as an entry point for their learning. An example of how popular culture can be brought into the classroom can be seen in Figure 8.1 where students were encouraged to visualise the relationship between Mary and a teenage Jesus in a contemporary context. Students wrote a short reflection to go with their image. As such, a dialogue between faith and culture is engaged, using stimulus that is relevant to the students' lives. The outcome is that the traditional narrative is contemporised and made meaningful for the student, who can then appreciate that older biblical or historical narratives can be reinvigorated via new tellings and interpretations.

Paul's letter to the Galatians: 3:28: *There is no longer Jew or Greek, there is no longer slave or free, there is no longer male or female; for all of you are one in Christ Jesus* effectively sums up the universalism of the Christian message, and the invitation to overcome differences, in order to dialogue in Christ. This is the outreach of the Catholic school today, despite a small growth of what may be seen as antagonism by some within the system. However, in a recent article Rossiter (2017) wonders if the use of the word 'Catholic' may in fact have a deleterious effect on the efficacy of the RE programme in schools and suggests that the programme may benefit from a diminution of particular nomenclature that may appear slightly coercive to the unconfessed. He writes:

> Some may not want to acknowledge the reality here, but the more the word 'Catholic' is used the more the activity is perceived as irrelevant. This is a principal reason why I think that the current emphasis on Catholic identity is counterproductive – it is not the label that RE really needs (Rossiter, 2017, p. 29).

There has been a growth in the recognition that our students need encounters that resonate with their own experience and the narratives in their own lives. This is confirmed by sociologist Phillip Hughes who writes that 'young people put life together themselves rather than following a predetermined way given to them by others' (p. 2) as quoted by Sharkey (2015). So, our task is to mediate our rich Tradition and the current times in ways that are meaningful and accessible to our students and in the hope that the Jesus narrative – the Good News – takes seed.

## A Culture of Dialogue

In relation to the importance of dialogue and its primacy in the education of, and between, all who attend a Catholic school, the recent Instruction from the Vatican, *The Identity of the Catholic School for a Culture of Dialogue,* January 2022, states:

> … it must therefore practise 'the grammar of dialogue' not as a technical expedient, but as a profound way of relating to others.… Pope Francis provided three fundamental guidelines to help dialogue, '… *the duty to respect one's own identity and that of others, the courage to accept differences, and sincerity of intentions. The duty to respect one's own identity and that of others*, because true dialogue cannot be built on ambiguity or a willingness to sacrifice some good for the sake of pleasing others. *The courage to accept differences*, because those who are different, either culturally or religiously, should not be treated as enemies, but rather treated as fellow-travellers, in the genuine conviction that the good of each resides in the good of all. *Sincerity of intentions*, because dialogue as an authentic expression of our humanity is not a strategy for achieving specific goals but rather a path to truth, one that deserves to be undertaken patiently, in order to transform competition into cooperation (para 30)'.

As we look to increasing the faith identity of the Catholic school, there are still challenges to overcome. Rossiter (2017) remarks that 'healthy Catholic school religious education needs to retain a creative tension between ecclesiastical concerns and the teacher's views about the spiritual and moral needs of pupils' (p.6). With the changing landscape of our schools, we must be aware of the push and pull of the Religious Education program and adapt it to benefit our students and to keep open the dialogue between our faith tradition, other traditions and emerging worldviews. As the pontiff reminds us, 'We cannot create a culture of dialogue if we do not have identity'. (Para 2, *The Identity of the Catholic for a Culture of Dialogue*). This is where our daily efforts to strengthen that identity are imperative. Perhaps we can keep in mind the notion that we are all fellow travellers and that in our Catholic schools, as we dialogue with each other – civilly, robustly, gently and respectfully – we prioritise the growth and good of all our students.

We also need to prioritise the growth in understanding of a diverse staff cohort which often reflects the various attitudes of the student population. In order to strengthen this identity, non-Catholic teaching staff at Catholic schools in Melbourne are required to gain 25 hours of professional learning within five years of being employed to achieve accreditation to teach in this sector. The new CECV (Catholic Education Commission of Victoria) policy (January 2020) follows a 'gain and maintain' trajectory After the initial five years the employee is required to undertake 25 hours of professional learning across three categories in each following five year period. The categories include the aims and objectives of the Catholic school; Catholic curriculum; Religious Education and faith development; and Catholic identity, culture, tradition and theology (including prayer, liturgy, Scripture and Catholic social teaching).

Many modules are often completed on staff spirituality/student-free days when all staff are mandated to gather to hear founding stories, new research, the unpacking of an encyclical, the latest on Church culture or to listen to a notable speaker on theology or spirituality. The various staff of congregational schools may gather together in one place so as to hear a uniform message. The sessions are approved for a number of hours by Melbourne Archdiocese Catholic Schools (MACS) and may be more general, or tailored specifically to the school's charism, history and culture. Many staff are happy to sit in an auditorium and passively listen, or to undertake an interactive workshop or reflective exercise. There is little demand made other than dutifully turning up. As with anything that one has to attend compulsorily, interest and attention are varied. Having conducted the occasional all-staff session, Ann has been gratified by those who smile or laugh or show active listening by nodding or asking questions. She has also seen people totally disengaged and on their phones and laptops, thereby making a mockery of the fact they will receive a participation certificate and an acknowledgement of the accredited hours.

Today in the education sector there is increasingly all sorts of compliance required of staff. This compliance includes undertaking mandatory reporting, disability and differentiation modules, as well as in-house professional learning that must be satisfied by staff. We must hope that the majority of staff is energised and engaged by learning about the school, its charism or elements of the Catholic faith tradition more generally, so that they can feel comfortable working in this context. Most manage to do so with good grace, but it would appear that there are a minority who are simply ticking the box and for whom the Catholic context is irrelevant to their teaching practice and worldview. With the honesty and anonymity of the ECSIP and SIF surveys, it is concerning if data indicates that there is a strong, albeit small, cluster of indifference, active dislike or cynicism about the Catholic model of education from those employed within the sector.

It will be interesting to see the 2023 ECSIP staff survey and what the data says about the overall attitude of teaching staff in the Catholic system or at a particular school. This will be especially the case in light of the recent MACS data about Catholic identity. This is a challenging area that we cannot afford to overlook. More than anything, students pick up on structure and consistency. They know the teachers who bother to pray in homerooms, the ones who respond appropriately in Mass, the ones who follow-up the Vinnies collection, the ones who know the liturgical season or the saint's day, whether Catholic or not. Consistency of modelling, in all areas of school life, is a priority for our students if they are to take away meaningful messages. If the enculturation of the Catholic context of the school is to be achieved, all staff must be on board with respect for the faith-based nature of the school, as they exercise their plurality in dialogue with the institution's ethos, vision and mission. If not an adherent (and that is absolutely fine) the teacher's disposition must be one that is intentionally and visibly open to the Catholic faith as one particular way of belonging and encountering the transcendent in community. This means that they need to be able to comfortably accept the charism and ethos of the school and work constructively within it.

As well as this, Catholic leadership density and succession needs to be in place so that changes at the top of the school do not impact deleteriously on the culture and practice of the school. Stability and consistency of practice across and through different leadership cycles are crucial if a vibrant, visible and welcoming Catholic school identity is to be maintained. This heralds the need for formation programs that enable and enrich leaders to feel confident in their faith leadership as a coherent programme is exercised to authentically anchor this dimension sector-wide.

## The new Religious Education Framework

The Religious Education Framework emerged in 2018 in draft format as a response to ECSIP for Catholic primary and secondary schools in the Melbourne Archdiocese. Its aims follow.

- Open up a more explicit dialogue between Catholic faith and the diverse cultures and lives of students.
- Find new ways to express the Gospel as alive and authentic.
- Engage in rich and meaningful experiences of prayer

The Framework drew on a new model for learning called 'The Pedagogy of Encounter'.

This model aimed to address the challenges of ECSIP, shifting schools from the lower quadrants of Figure 8.2 to the top right quadrant – the Dialogue School. The heart of the model is student lives and questions, with dialogue rather than explicit teaching as the process. It responds to the times in a recontextualisation model that acknowledges the impact of social change and new tranches of thought. Students are encouraged to respond to provocations that teachers present about particular issues. They are asked to think about the issue, do some research to find out what others think and why, and then consider these in the light of Catholic Church teaching. The personal response of students and how their perspective might have changed throughout this time conclude the process. It is a process that challenges the students to question their own perceptions and to stretch their understanding in response to new learnings. Ultimately, 'A pedagogy of encounter acknowledges the grace of God at work in the teachings of the Church, in learning relationships, and particularly in dialogue' (REC Framework, 2018, p. 8).

Somewhat similar to *To Know Worship and Love*, the key learning areas in the new Framework are:

- Scripture and Jesus
- Church and Community
- God, Religion and Life
- Sacrament, Prayer and Liturgy
- Morality and Justice

However, the approach is very different to this earlier text. Units often consist more of questions rather than topics. For example:

- Was Jesus a Christian or a Jew?
- Should victims of crime forgive those who act against them?
- Did Hitler go to heaven?
- What should we do with all the poor people? (MacKillop College, Werribee, Year 8).

Further, lessons tend to focus on inquiry, rather than solely on explicit instruction, and involve a collaborative approach where peer-to-peer learning is fostered. As experienced teachers, we know how vital this learning is and how important it is for the cross-fertilisation in thinking that happens when students can bounce ideas off each other, sometimes without the teacher hovering and directing. In the following section we will share examples of how this has occurred in the schools we have worked in over recent years.

## Exploring the Religious Education Framework

As a Religious Education leader at the Senior Campus of Xavier College, Bernadette had the opportunity to introduce a Pedagogy of Encounter to Year 9 teachers. The unit that we initially revised was the Catholic Church in Australia unit from *To Know, Worship and Love Year 9.* An inquiry unit was collaboratively developed (Appendix 1) which allowed students to wonder about the story of the Church in Australia after the teacher had presented a brief overview from early convict days to the present day. Students worked in small groups with butcher's paper to brainstorm an unGoogleable question that they would research, such as why do we consider Mary MacKillop a saint or why was St Francis' Church in Melbourne's city centre built and why is it still an important place for Catholics today? After a number of lessons of research, students prepared a presentation for the class and

Figure 8.1: A contemporary image of Mary's relationship with Jesus as a teenager by a Xavier student, 2017.

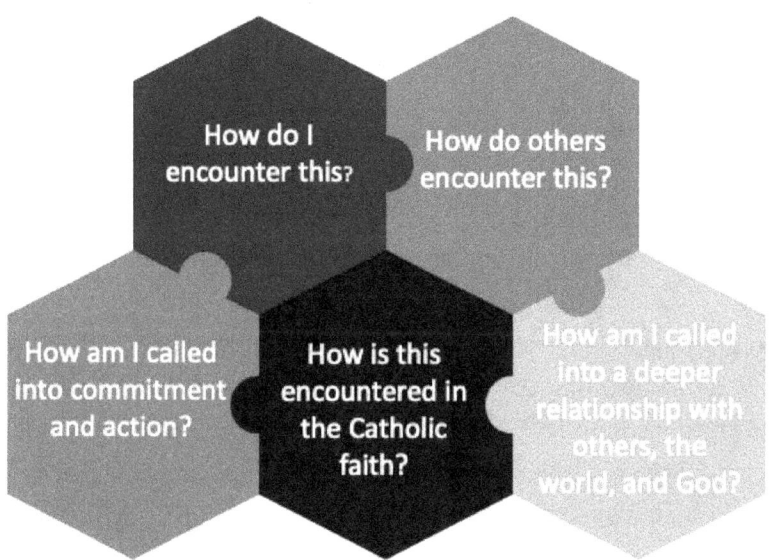

Diagram 8.3: Pedagogy of Encounter (ReSource, 2022)

took turns to share their findings. Overall, this was a very successful unit, and provided students with arguably a much deeper appreciation of the story of the Catholic Church in Australia than four to five weeks of explicit instruction would have provided. The role of the educator in this context is as the facilitator of learning, rather than 'sage on the stage' and students move from passive recipients of knowledge to active participants in their own learning (Morrison, 2014, p. 1).

It seems that the Year 9 Religious Education class is fertile ground for experimentation and trial. The students at this year-level often have alternative educational programs, separate campuses and immersion days to stimulate learning and to project ideas for future pathways and interests. Before the tightening of the timetable for VCE and the adoption of learning patterns for success in that setting, Year 9 is a year for adventure and experiment. At Genazzano, one of the most successful units calls on the creation of a personal Creed. We start the lessons with a general provocation as to what the girls believe about themselves and their interaction with the world. Questions for the girls might be: *What do you stand for? What won't you stand for? When are you angry or upset by structural issues? Do you feel heard?* This comes down to some existential questioning: Why are you here? What is the purpose of your life? What will you do with it? Who and what do you believe in? A whole constellation of ideas come together, sometimes bombarding the students, sometimes sneaking up on them. All those questions - and occasional answers - that they are trying on for size and fit as they mature and find their place in the world. We may listen to recent songs, such as Savage Garden's 'Affirmation' or that old favourite 'I Believe' and interrogate the lyrics. The girls often have suggestions that are relevant, resonant and up-to-date! They know the words and music. Careful letting go and giving the students creative control energises their efforts and responses. Using popular culture and situating lessons where the students are, assists in making what they do personally meaningful.

Then we do formal background work on the Nicene Creed, why it was formulated and when. This information comes from *To Know Worship and Love* and is delivered in more of teacher-instructive mode. This in turn provides an historical and theological window into its formulation and a renewed understanding of a prayer that can be recited unthinkingly sometimes, but is ultimately a prayer that binds Catholics in a recognisably shared belief that is globally unifying. Other sources and commentary are also used. After that, we go through the statements themselves and flesh them out so that theological nuances are understood. Here, the students can ask questions, contest and challenge. After that, we look at various mission and vision statements of institutions and what they promise. Then we ask the girls to devise their creedal statement; a statement that intersperses their own personal beliefs with their spiritual or religious ones. A model is shared with them as a starting point for their own efforts (Appendix 2). I suggest to the girls that their personal creed is their own mission and vision statement; it encapsulates their attitudes and behaviours, the way they see and respond to the world around them as fifteen-year-olds. It is their own unique worldview combined with the sacred and the secular. The girls write this up and then read it to the class. The responses from their peers are appreciative and positive, perhaps because the girls are telling their truths.

This has been one of the most gratifying units I have encountered. The responses are so often prayerful and poetic, alive with the spirit of each writer and what matters to them. They are often brimming with hope, their spirituality writ large and often a nod to the Catholic community and its teachings. It is a wide and deep look at who they are and who they would like to be in the light of their own faith and their growing realisation of their agency for the common good.

Sometimes, I suggest that they put this creed in their treasure/memory box so that they can look back on it in later years. In doing so they will see how this creedal statement may have confirmed much of who they are or it may signpost how they have changed over the course of time and experience. From a teacher's perspective, these beautiful articulations of faith and life reinforce everything hopeful about the next generation and the attitudes and intentions that will guide them as stewards of the future.

## Prayer

One of the distinguishing features of the Catholic school is the primacy of prayer. It is not simply an add-on, but central to a sense of belonging and identity and the richness of our Judeo-Christian heritage. The power and potency of prayer and the time given to do it properly, whether in homeroom, during an RE lesson or in a school-wide Eucharistic celebration, is a life-enhancing gift of grace to the student. Whether it be through Special Intentions in class; formal Prayers of the Faithful at Mass; the Examen, Taizé or other conduits to enlarging our personal relationship with God; we begin to co-create the prayerful experience the moment we submit ourselves to union with the Trinity.

Prayer feeds the soul. In a world of instant gratification, we need the pause and ponder of prayer to give us spiritual ballast. Prayer can make us look at the world and its wonders – and woes – in new, deep, discerning and hopeful ways. Prayer is about surrendering time and ego. It is about going in, soul-searching, and not being afraid to seek what it is we need from God, and from ourselves. As models to our students, we need to let them see us pray with reverence and respect and with a disposition that suggests that nothing goes unanswered.

According to the *Catechism of the Catholic Church* (534) prayer is the 'raising of one's heart and mind to God.' In this encounter one enters a personal relationship with God and joins with all those past and present – the communion of saints – who have prayed with similar fidelity and earnestness in the Catholic community.

The Benedictine nun, Joan Chittister, reminds us that prayer is an attitude of mind, a quality of soul and a dimension of the daily. Prayerful habituation can only grow us into better people. Once we have stilled and readied ourselves, wherever we gather is transfigured, albeit briefly, into a sacred space. We have decentralised ourselves in readiness for the prayerful encounter. Prayer is our pause point in the middle of all we must do.

Our private prayer is our resting in God and letting him into the secrets of our successes and sorrows, our doubts and delights, letting him in, unconditionally, no ifs or buts or maybes. Our public prayer confirms our identity as a worshipping community, especially when we recite those well-loved and well-worn prayers such as the 'Our Father', the 'Hail Mary' or the decades of rosary, common to Catholics across the globe. In Luke's Gospel Jesus tells his disciples a parable about their need to pray always and never lose heart (Luke 18:1) In the 21st century, in a world saturated by competing demands, the act of praying is almost counter-cultural in an age which sometimes disparages or sidelines the religious or spiritual impulse.

Praying together as a staff group enhances that sense of community cohesion and collegiality. It is an act of faith. Sometimes our prayers flow from harmony and other times from disquiet. We respond to the world as it is beamed into us, in its moments of rapture and beauty and in its moments of interruption and discontinuity. This is especially so for our students whose life experience may mean that they are emotionally brittle or anxious. As the adults in the room, it is always up to us to be aware of situations that may evoke prayer and to discern the appropriateness of that prayer, especially if that prayer may appear to alienate or disqualify others (inadvertently or otherwise) in a multicultural classroom.

And sometimes in prayer we just have to listen, quieten, slow, pause and stop to finally hear the silence that brims with hope and restoration. Other other times the prayer may be more inventive.

In a state of adoration we might conjure ideas that can turn our hearts and minds to new ways of thinking. In a mode of supplication we can create prompts for change. In an overwhelm of gratitude we can forge a new humility. In a place of contrition we can promise commitment. On occasion, the epiphany of startling new *knowing* opens up the soul in a regenerative burst of goodness and *being*.

As we model a prayer life for our students we are reminded of the importance of authenticity of witness. We pray because we believe. Mindful, too, of the composition of our classes today we are reminded of the unique spiritual space that is Catholic. We invite those who think differently to contribute as they feel comfortable. In the classroom, believers of other faith traditions or no tradition may reflect or contribute in an atmosphere of hospitality and reciprocity, whereby the Catholic student is enriched by this dialogue as they affirm their own faith tradition.

With prayer as central to the life of the school, it is imperative that the time taken to pray is honoured. It should not be rushed or hurried, as part of its quiet energy is a natural slowing down and dispositional readiness for those who pray. We know that prayers must be age-and stage-appropriate and that the right setting can help orient the student to the sacred moment. We also know that prayer can bring a community together in both happy and sad times. It is the grace and glue of connection, sometimes a shorthand in faith that we come to rely on when our own words are not enough. Prayer can often be a symbol of solidarity – when we say we are praying for someone, or when we collectively pray for those in situations where we cannot intervene directly to help. I know my students, recognising that children their age in the Ukraine were having their lives dreadfully disrupted during the unlawful invasion of the country, wanted to be with them in prayer. So, too, during the ravages of Covid 19 and the aftermath of 9/11. Sometimes, we come to prayer with the weight of the world on our shoulders, burdens almost too heavy to bear, hearts empty, perhaps feeling spiritually absent. The desire to connect with God, even though feeling negative, is why prayer is so essential to our spiritual wellbeing.

In a multitasking, fragmented world, prayer is a single spiritual task that is unique and special to each person who prays. How fortunate are we in our Catholic schools that we have the opportunity to make time for the sacred, to build both the individual student's soul and the institutional soul of our community.

For that blessed breathing space in the busyness of all our lives we are truly grateful. Amen.

# References

2016 Census, Australian Bureau of Statistics.

Boeve, L, 'Religious education in a post-secular and post-Christian', *Journal of Beliefs & Values*, 33:2, 2012, pp. 143-156, doi.10.1080/13617672.2012.694058

Boeve, 'Horizon: The challenge of plurality and difference', *Theology at the crossroads of university, church and society : dialogue, difference and Catholic identity*, T&T Clark, Bloomsbury, 2016, pp. 33 - 53.

Catholic Education Conference Victoria (CECV), *Victorian Catholic Schools Statistics at a Glance*, 2019.Cardinal Joseph Versaldi, 'Congregation for Catholic Education (for Educational Institutions)', The Identity of the Catholic School for a Culture of Dialogue, January 25, 2022.'

Chambers, M, 'Students who are not Catholics in Catholic schools: lessons from the Second Vatican Council about the Catholicity of schools', *International Studies in Catholic Education*, 4:2, 2012, pp. 186-199, doi: 10.1080/19422539.2012.708174.

Flynn, M, *The Culture of Catholic Schools: A study of Catholic Schools 1972 -1993*, St Pauls, 1993.

Fowler, JW, *Stages in Faith: The Psychology of Human Development and the Quest for Meaning*, Harper Row, New York, 1981.

Gowdie, J, *Stirring the Soul of Catholic Education. Formation for Mission*, Vaughan Publishing, 2017.

Horner, R, 'Enhancing Catholic School Identity through Religious Education', Conference paper, Australian Catholic University, 2020.

Mackay, H, *Beyond Belief*, Pan MacMillan Australia, 2016.

MacKillop College, Werribee. Retrieved from: https://www.mackillopwerribee.com.au/learning-teaching/2022-curriculum-handbooks/

Morrison, (2014), 'From 'Sage on the Stage' to 'Guide on the Side': A Good Star', *International Journal for the Scholarship of Teaching and Learning*, 8(1). DOI:10.20429/ijsotl.2014.080104

National Centre for Pastoral Research (NCPR), Catholic Bishops Conference (2021, 2021), National Count of Attendance at Mass and Sunday Assemblies.

National Count of Attendance (2006, 2011), National Church Life Survey 2006 and 2011.

RE Curriculum Framework, 2018, accessed from https//resource-macs.com/wp-/content/uploads/2018/09/RE-Curr-Framework-Jan-2018.pdfRossiter, G, in *Religion in Australian Catholic Schools: Exploring the Landscape*, edited by R Rymarz and A Belmonte, Garratt Publishing, 2017.

Rymarz, R and Hyde, B, *Taking the next step: Teaching religious education in Catholic schools*, David Barlow Publishing, Macksville, NSW, 2013.

Rymarz, R and Sharkey, P, *Moving from Theory to Practice*, Vaughan Publishing, 2019.

Sharkey, P, *Educators Guide to Catholic Identity*. Garratt Publishing, 2015.

Sheridan, G, *God is Good for You: A Defence of Christianity in Troubled Times*, Allen & Unwin, 2018.

Windsor, G, *The Tempest-Tossed Church*, New South Publications, 2017.

## Reflection

1. What evidence can you provide for the increasing secularisation of Australian society?
2. Is there still a role for Catholic schools today?
3. What type of Catholic school did you attend (if any) in terms of the ECSI model? Provide some examples.
4. What do you see as the advantages of the Pedagogy of Encounter as a way of teaching Religious Education? Are there any disadvantages?
5. Pope Francis noted that we live not only in an era of change, but a change of era. How do you see this impacting in the classroom and for the future direction of the RE curriculum and the viability/agency of faith-based schools in a culture of secularisation?
6. How do we continue to evangelise authentically in a world of invasive and competing demands and attractions?
7. Do we need to revitalise or restate our various schools' vision and mission in response to the world as it is today? What suggestions or ideas do you have?
8. How can the Catholic worldview intersect positively and creatively with the reality of teenage lives today? Ideas? Suggestions? Innovations?
9. Is 'mission drift' a reality in your school?
10. What does leadership need to acknowledge, do or change so that the Catholic identity of the school is prioritised?
11. How do we build confidence in the next generation of leaders and teachers in the Catholic system?
12. Take some time – take it now – to pause and pray about your role in the active mission of the Church.

Figure 9.1: Celebrating the Eucharist in the Genazzano chapel

# CHAPTER NINE
## Current Issues

*A dialogue school bridges the gap between faith and culture, responding to the times, whilst ensuring the gospel imperative unapologetically informs the school's ethos and practice*
(Horner, 2020, p. 7)

As the last chapter indicated, there are new and exciting directions in the way Religious Education (RE) is envisaged by the Melbourne and other dioceses. Schools are encouraged to move towards being Dialogue Schools where students can actively engage with their faith as they grapple with global issues. Teachers, in turn, are called to be 'witnesses, specialists and moderators' – *witnesses* in terms of having established a religious identity for themselves, *specialists* in having background in key areas such as scripture and theology, and *moderators* in terms of being able to facilitate dialogue in the classroom (Pollefeyt, 2008).

In order to facilitate this and to keep the integrity of Religious Education as a discipline in its own right, there are some school-based challenges that need to be addressed. Just as there is a misapprehension that all teachers are English teachers, there is an attitude in some schools that RE can be taught by anyone. Sometimes, it is as simple as the making-up of a teacher's load. And how often have we seen advertisements on the professional pages for teaching appointments in other subjects and the added line – *ability to teach RE an advantage*. Already RE is relegated to the role of add-on. There are occasions when teachers who are not Catholic, but religiously predisposed, have taught classes. There are also occasions when a teacher with no faith background has taught a class. They have done a fabulous job as history teachers in RE, but the faith or witness dimension has been totally absent.

We know that many schools have teachers who are teaching out of their area. For example, 40 per cent of Maths teachers in Australia (2022) do not have that subject as their university discipline. This is also happening in RE. As a consequence the depth of knowledge, familiarity with Church teaching and tradition, scripture and theology, and the ability to respond to the questions asked by students, may be vastly different because of teacher expertise and experience. This is a matter of fairness across a year level that may have multiple classes. The quality, depth and ability to engage the class is crucial in RE. This is particularly the case with wider cross-contextual, relevant and topical elements. It is also a matter both of professionalism and justice in that the students deserve to have a well-qualified – and the best teacher possible – in RE, or in any other subject for that matter. Short-changing our students in any subject undermines the whole educational project and the possibility of potential growth, flourishing and mastery in that area.

Operational matters in the school should not undermine the primacy of Religious Education – especially as this goes to the *raison dêtre* of the school's existence. There is concern when a teacher, and especially a new teacher to RE, is told by a member of the school leadership that there are few corrections in RE compared to other subjects. Saying this suggests that the subject is not taken seriously or is 'lightweight' and that anyone can do it. This is simply not the case, especially at VCE level. Fobbing a teacher off with the old 'RE is an easy gig' line is just not true and needs to be nipped in the bud. The last thing the Catholic sector needs is enthusiastic young teachers being overloaded and overwhelmed. This is also the case when RE is marginalised as not important by an executive team who have no idea about the subject, have never taught it, and see it as faith-based frippery. This derisory and blinkered attitude towards the subject that is foundational to the school needs to be addressed if the promotion of the Catholic identity of the school is to be ongoing and transformative. This goes to the heart of the appointments made at the leadership level.

The three aspects of *witness, specialist* and *moderator* are required attributes for the contemporary RE teacher. With these attributes, the teacher can create a classroom that is engaging, challenging and nurturing of the spiritual growth of the student. Authentic engagement in the RE class is where the teacher accompanies students as they make their way to meaning, a journey that is unique and idiosyncratic. Treston (2001) describes this growth as a 'spiritual homecoming to true self' (p. 53).

*Lay Catholics in Schools* (1982) states:

> The more completely an education can give concrete witness to the model of the ideal person that is being presented to the students, the more this ideal will be believed and imitated. For it will then be seen as something reasonable and worthy of being lived, something concrete and realizable. It is in this context that the faith witness of the lay teacher becomes especially important. Students should see in their teacher the Christian attitude and behaviour that is often so conspicuously absent from the secular atmosphere in which they live. Without this witness, living in such an atmosphere, they may begin to regard Christian behaviour as an impossible ideal' ( Para. 32).

We have the 'privileged opportunity' (LC, Para. 33) to witness who we are in all our interactions, and this witness must be credible and inviting for our students. What they see in us may well be subtly internalised; often the bud that will bloom later. We offer the lesson of ourselves to our students in the hope that they see the Christian ideal as possible. We create the space for our students to seek, to soul search, to become. The RE classroom with its room for deep thinking, meditation, prayer and reflection, as well as robust and contested discussion on all manner of ethical subjects, builds capacities such as discernment, curiosity, critical appreciation and, most importantly, the inclusive dialogue that becomes the framework for adult life.

However, the reality is that in many schools there is not a ready supply of the expert RE teachers that Pollefeyt (2008) envisages, even though many are willing and do everything they can to engage students. With classrooms that house students from a variety of backgrounds and with varying degrees of interest in RE, teaching is not always an easy task, especially for those not specifically trained. As Cullen (2019) pertinently asks, 'If the religion teacher is to undertake the task of educating others for this purpose, then it is appropriate to ask if they are religiously educated themselves' (p. 75). She goes on to argue for explicit religious education for teachers – to both initially train them and to support their ongoing development. Similarly, Dowling (2012) challenges those responsible for professional learning within the Catholic sector to offer frequent opportunities for RE teachers to learn from each other collaboratively, as well as seeking support from other schools or outside agencies. She suggests that 'external top down reforms are often compliance driven and viewed as "off the shelf", process driven and generalised' (p. 25). In other words, they tick boxes, but may not value-add in the area of specialist growth.

Dowling (2012) suggests we should move to continuous 'self review' where teachers meet regularly with those in their teams with the aim of improving student outcomes (p, 25). This is similar to the thinking of Wenger-Trayner et al. (2020) who speak of 'learning loops' where teachers learn about new strategies in a Community of Practice (CoP)/Personal Learning Team (PLT), trial them in their classroom, and then return to the CoP/PLT to share successes and failures with others who have experimented in their own classrooms. In terms of RE, this would be an ideal way of implementing the Religious Education Framework, and, in particular, the Pedagogy of Encounter. For teachers who have been used to working primarily from a textbook such as *To Know, Worship and Love*, this is a new way of engaging with students. Working collaboratively is a preferred model of learning, rather than passively listening to a presentation or attending a conference, and not having the opportunity to share the learning gained there. However, this type of learning for RE teachers requires dedicated time and skilled leadership and facilitation. Facilitation rests with the role of the Religious Education Coordinator (REC) or other skilled facilitator in a school.

*The Catholic School on the Threshold of the Third Millennium* states that the Catholic School is a place of integral education of the human person through a clear educational project of which Christ is the foundation: it is also a project directed at creating a synthesis between faith, culture and life (Par. 4). This integral, holistic, generative process is the quest for an education which is faith and life-enhancing and recognises that all lives, most especially those of our students, are lived in the context of the contemporary cultural crucible. In a Catholic school the role of the Religious Education Coordinator (REC) is crucial as it can shape how the curriculum is animated and delivered, both from a school-based imperative and in response to diocesan directives. How this is done can reflect the expertise, energy and enthusiasm of the staff and the impact and effect of this subject, as it is received by the student cohort. This, in turn, is a mirror of the Catholic identity of a school. It also reflects whether this is a lived reality or whether there has been some diminution of that identity through: external circumstances, leadership, timetable or budget constraints, and/or student demographic and age. All this can be gauged by the ECSIP data. This data can be impacted significantly at the classroom level by the quality of teaching and learning that takes place in Religious Education. Data can also identify the degree of Catholicity in a school through the opportunities offered by liturgical or sacramental celebrations, morning or homeroom prayer and gathering as a believing community for a feast day, founder's day or for Easter or Christmas Eucharist.

The importance of the appointment of an REC, under the direction of the Principal and/or Board, cannot be underestimated. This appointment is crucial to the faith life of the school, the agency of the RE team, and their sense of collegial cohesion in working together vocationally to educate the young bodies and souls before them. This person must be, firstly, a person of conviction for whom the championing of the religious life of the school is integral to the job they do, and to how they see themselves doing that job well. And it is more than a job, always; more perhaps a mission as they navigate the cultural waters of school, the diversity of its staff and students, the bureaucratic, educational and ecclesial expectations of the role, its administration and leadership, its complexity, and the changing shape and demands of the subject, especially in schools where all disciplines battle for primacy and a fair allocation in the timetable. As Buchanan (2014) notes, the role of the REC is a relatively new one, and has no distinct or homogenous definition, in its application across the twenty-eight Catholic dioceses in Australia.

The role of the REC is not for the faint of heart. The REC in most schools works under, or is answerable to, the Deputy Principal: Faith and Mission (or a person with a similar title) so it is imperative that these two people have a good working relationship, and confidence in each other's expertise and that of their staff. They must share a congruence of vision for the religious life of the school. Whilst the

DP may have a more public role, it is the REC who oversees the curriculum and the daily teaching and learning that takes place in the school. This is an arduous job, especially with the increasing demands of administration and documentation, the managerial aspects of tending to a diversity of staff, varying degrees of qualification of that staff, and the engagement of the said staff as colleagues with the same mission or purpose in mind as they undertake their teaching.

Buchanan (2014, p. 15) notes that one of the realities of the experience of the REC, as well as the Deputy Principal in the faith domain, is that as leaders in the school, they occasionally feel sidelined when the ministerial aspect of their job, such as organising Eucharistic celebrations, reflection days, retreats and other spiritually-formative days, does not appear to have the same significance as those disciplines which are more overtly content driven. This is one of the tensions that exists in the Catholic school where RE can be seen as less academically valuable than other disciplines, despite the quality of teaching and results in Year 12 examinations.

An REC must be a person of faith and that faith must be visible. They must be prophetic in their purpose. They are servant leaders, invested in the position not for personal aggrandisement or authority, but because they have a profound connection to the faith and want to ensure that this is lived out as a daily reality in the school for all to see and experience. This goes to the authenticity of their leadership. A truly authentic REC will ennoble and empower those around them to be their best selves. They will be encouragers of their team, building up professional and personal capacity so that the RE staff see themselves as central and integral to the core being of their Catholic school. The authentic REC does not work alone. They lead and are part of a professional community that is built on goodwill, competence, mutuality and reciprocity. As a leader, the REC should develop a personal resilience or 'hardiness' (Evans, 1996, p. 193) so that they can weather the turbulence of resistance and change. According to Evans, a leader must 'build their practice outward from their core commitments rather than inward from a management text' (p. 193). The REC must be a faith leader first and a manager second. A good leader is direction setting, builds healthy relationships, manages change strategically, deprivatises and shares new knowledge, and embeds consistency in pedagogic and administrative structures. The effective blending of these components enables the REC to build followership in their own department and expand this more widely through the school community.

Our experience has been that RE departments often comprise the same people over many years. These staff all have their own way of teaching, their own preferences as to year levels and content ownership, and may have their own way of seeing how RE is connected to the school, congruent more generally with the collective approach, but perhaps with an individual key. This has implications for how an REC introduces new ideas.

The imposition of new directives or revised or updated material or a new school management system requires the REC to negotiate with staff gently so that they all feel a part of the journey of change or adaptation. The REC also needs to recognise that the staff have capabilities that should be utilised and these should be acknowledged and celebrated. The REC, as a good leader, should also be aware of those areas where a teacher is not comfortable or not equipped or competent in some area. For example, some RE staff in secondary schools are on the older side and may not be as digitally capable as younger staff – or indeed their own classes. Some staff may need further professional development in areas such as the history of the Church or biblical familiarity. Some staff may not feel comfortable taking classes on respectful relationships and human sexuality. This particular aspect of Church teaching is often co-taught under a health and wellbeing banner. This banner will often reflect the changes of puberty: the increasing sexualisation found in much entertainment, advertising and social media; and love in the context of the commitment of marriage.

Schools have a responsibility to provide information and cannot abrogate this because they do not like the content or it contradicts Church doctrine. Consent is a new area that needs expert and sensitive delivery. We now have gender transitioning and LGBTQ or LGBTQIA+ identifying students and they have a rightful place at our schools. The dilemma for those who teach senior RE is the school's upholding of traditional Church teaching, its primacy, and the recognition that many older students have views and experiences that deem the more traditional views outdated. Here we are reminded that we have bodies as well as souls in front of us and we must navigate this path with care and compassion.

The REC stands up for the gospel imperative as being foundational to the ethos of the school and its lived reality. Their leadership should model this for all to see. This is not to expect an inordinate standard of piety, but instead the warm outreach that includes others and brings them along supportively on the journey of evangelisation of their students. George (2003) suggests there is no normative style for leadership, and that an REC might need to adapt their leadership approach to the particular situational context they find themselves in. An effective REC understands the need to use a wide repertoire of skills to successfully accomplish change, or innovation, or a refreshing of the founding charism. In concert with the Principal and the Deputy Principal, they may have a vision to accomplish a goal which moves the whole community from the current reality to the imagined future. This may also involve the counter-culturalism which Jesus exercised, the critiquing of structures and attitudes which demean rather than dignify what it is to be a human being made in the image of God.

The REC is in a position to make the most of good connections with other RECs whose schools may be studying the same text, have shared social justice initiatives, wish to hear from an international speaker, or have a connecting charism which could be explored more roundly on shared reflection days. We were both fortunate in our early days of being an REC to connect with other Melbourne RECs on a regular basis. Our days were facilitated and involved much sharing and fellowship. The fostering of this mutuality among RECs can bring multiple benefits sector wide; the exchange of ideas; and the imagination, energy and enthusiasm to devise new approaches or strategies in the RE programme. They may also offer wisdom, insight and understanding of the multitudinous tasks that are above and beyond a mere role description. Schools can also connect via their shared charism which may mean that international schools can connect not just on sporting tours or overseas visits, but also at the level of founding spirituality. Here participants can observe how the charism is activated differently because of circumstance, language or place, whilst still remaining elementally and steadfastly the same.

Authentic leadership must be professionally effective. Thus the REC, as well as being competent in their discipline, combined with the associated credibility this provides, must engage in their sphere of influence and participate in subject associations such as the Texts and Traditions Teachers Association or the Religious and Society network (RASNET). This can build their professional knowledge, dialogue with others doing similar work in other schools, and enhance and grow a sense of collegiality and purpose beyond the school to a more systemic involvement in the mission of the Catholic school. Such connections can facilitate a range of important outcomes. These may include discussion with other teachers, beneficial cross-marking and moderation with staff from other schools, shared material, lectures and visits by theologians (for example, Brendan Byrne SJ coming to speak on the themes of hospitality in Luke's Gospel for a Texts class), and special revision talks for the students prior to the exams. As this book is being published, Bernadette is now a Study Specialist

Reviewer (having been an examiner for many years) for the Victorian Curriculum and Assessment Association (VCAA), editing exams and ensuring that their language is accessible to students.

Networking is different for everyone. For the REC it is not about business cards, glad-handing and free drinks. Rather it's about professional learning, inspiration and looking at the world of faith and culture more widely. In her efforts, Ann has presented at RE conferences and undertaken staff days at other schools on topics such as prayer and the spirituality of the teacher. As part of her engagement professionally and personally, Ann was commissioned to write a book, *Grit and Grace* (David Lovell Publishing, 2014) on the foundress of the Faithful Companions of Jesus, the aforementioned Marie Madeleine d'Houët, and has since that time been working with Garratt Publishing in writing and compiling annual prayer and reflection resources for Australasian teachers. In 2018, Ann scripted and recorded 40 five-minute episodes with the international group Shalom Media in a series for primary students entitled *The Little Way of Lent*. She did her own hair and make-up! She writes a national column in *Australian Catholics*, contributes to other mainstream media and writes a monthly column for a group of local parishes. Ann has published two books for the Catholic and general reader; *The Secret Garden of Spirituality: Reflections on Faith, Life and Education* (Michelle Anderson Publishing, 2011) and *Blessed: Meditations on a Life of Small Wonders* (Laneway Press, 2021). Somewhere in this effort, Ann has identified that her love of writing is something of a calling when it comes to issues of faith. She has her models; Joan Chittister OSB, the Benedictine nun who is something of a spiritual warrior: John O'Donoghue, the Irish poet/philosopher and American writer Brian Doyle, whose writing is simply heavenly. That is not to say that Ann is preternaturally pious. She has also written about Elvis and poetry and Paris and the simple joys of living. Perhaps she is seeing God in all things!

Bernadette has moved in other directions by doing sessional teaching at the Australian Catholic University with both secondary and primary pre-service teachers as a lecturer and tutor of Religious Education. This sessional teaching has provided a great opportunity to form the next generation of RE teachers, and doing so with a focus on the Pedagogy of Encounter, the teacher as moderator, and ways of making RE lively and interesting for students. She also went on to complete a PhD which, although more generally in education, had application in RE in terms of exploring ways that teachers could collaborate in Communities of Practice to improve student learning. The latter culminated in the publication of her co-authored book, *Sustaining Early Career Teacher Communities of Practice* (Mercieca & McDonald, 2021). She was also fortunate to travel to Israel in 2013 on a parish pilgrimage and to Russia in 2018 for a Russian Icon tour. These were wonderful experiences and provided great photos to use in RE classes!

So these two young Catholic girls from Chapter One have come quite a distance in terms of their ventures and achievements. They still have much to offer and to do.

# References

Buchanan, M, *Religious Education Leadership and the 21st Century: Overcoming Disconnectedness*, ejournal of Catholic Education in Australasia, 2014.

Cullen, S, 'The Religious Education of the Religious Education Teacher in Catholic Schools', *Global Perspectives on Catholic Religious Education in Schools. Volume II, Learning and Leading in a Pluralist World*, Springer, Singapore: https://doi.org/10.1007/978-981-13-6127-2.

Dowling, E, 'An investment in our future: Reimagining professional learning for religious educators', *Journal of Religious Education*, 2012.

Evans, R, 'Authentic Leader', *The Human Side of School Change: Reform, Resistance and the Real Life Problems of Innovation*, Jossey-Bass, San Francisco, 1966.

George, B, 'Leadership is authenticity, not style, *Authentic leadership: Rediscovering the secrets of creating lasting value*, Jossey-Bass, San Francisco, 2003.

Mercieca, B and McDonald, J, *Sustaining Communities of Practice with Early Career Teachers*, Springer, 2021.

Pollefeyt, D, 'Difference Matters. A Hermeneutic-Communicative Concept of Didactics of Religion in a European Multi-Religious Context', *Journal of Religious Education, 56* (1), 2008.

Treston, K, *Wisdom Schools – Seven pillars of Wisdom for Catholic schools*, Creation Enterprises, Brisbane, 2001.

'Lay Catholics in Schools: Witnesses to Faith', *Congregation for Catholic Education* (1982).

'The Catholic School on the Threshold of the Third Millennium', *Congregation for Catholic Education*, 1997.

Wenger-Trayner, E and Wenger-Trayner, B, *Learning to Make a Difference: Value Creation in Social Learning Spaces*, Cambridge University Press. 2020, doi:10.1017/9781108677431

## Reflection

1. Can you authentically witness your Catholic faith to students? What might you need to support you so that you feel confident and competent in delivering an RE programme?
2. How do you see RE perceived at your school? By non-RE staff? By students? By parents?
3. What qualities do you think are integral to the role of REC? To the role of Deputy Principal: Faith and Mission?
4. Is the faith life of your school visible and seen as central to its existence?
5. What can you offer as an RE teacher today?

## CHAPTER TEN
## Future Prospects

*We are educating today for tomorrow, not today for yesterday*
(Rymarz & Sharkey, 2019, p. 130).

We do not have a crystal ball. Yet we both have experiences in Catholic secondary schools and Catholic higher education over many years. This experience has given us insights into what the future might look like, and what strategies we might recommend to make it an authentic future for Catholic schools. We are aware of the challenges that face Catholic education, as articulated by Boeve (2012), for example, where:

> … on the one hand it cares for the future of the Christian tradition, and on the other hand it wants to live up to a context that steadily recedes from the Christian culture and that pluralises religiously (p. 155).

We are also mindful that our generation of Baby-Boomers will be leaving the RE classroom in the next few years and that teachers belonging to Gen X, Gen Y and the Millennial demographic will take our place. Their experience of growing up Catholic is different to ours and that difference will be exercised in the classrooms of tomorrow. As Gowdie (2017) reminds us, these younger cohorts, especially the Millennials, are a generation of seekers, and whilst institutions may not have their loyalty, they value authentic behaviour and conduct. As such, we older RE teachers are in a position to advise and mentor in this communal project. As RE teachers we join many others in seeking a Church response to the revised meaning-making that makes sense to the generations that follow us. We recognise the importance of new ways of formation. We understand that the spiritual capital and its resourcing needed to keep the Catholic education project is revelatory, and relevant, for those in the contemporary classroom – both teacher and student.

Our recommendations focus on the three main areas that frame this book: Witness, Specialist and Moderator.

## Witness

Our concern as experienced educators is that once our generation retires, as they are increasingly doing, there will be a dearth of qualified Religious Education (RE) educators with a strong faith background. We do not make this claim lightly but base it on the statistics which were shown in Chapter 8. Following are the stats for those prospective RE teachers born post 1994.

Less than 1 per cent are core Catholics – who go to Church at least monthly and formally belong to a Church community. There are 24 per cent first generation unchurched and 45 per cent second generation unchurched (Boeve, 2016). In light of this we call for a number of measures.

The first is for active succession planning to attract the smaller proportions of young school leavers who do show an interest in Religious Education. This could include schools offering scholarships to these students to study theology, scripture and/or religious education as part of their academic studies at university. There are a number of universities that offer this option. These students would, in turn, be obliged to return to their school for some – though not all – placements and then their first teaching position. This is not unlike the old government sponsored studentships some of us had in the 1970s and 1980s, and not dissimilar to the incentives governments are currently offering to Maths and Science students in terms of reduced fees. Such succession planning is an indicator of systemic good health and positive functionality, a necessary building block for preserving and strengthening teacher capacity and sustainable future leadership that will contribute to the maintenance of an integral Catholic identity.

It is pleasing to note that there has been some movement in this area. The following announcement was noted on the CathNews website on 17/6/2022.

> Catholic Education, Diocese of Wagga Wagga (CEDWW) is offering five scholarships to current year 12 students in Catholic schools who intend to begin an undergraduate course in teacher training in 2023. The scholarships will see successful applicants gain a total benefit of up to $20,000 per recipient, paid as $5000 for each year successfully completed. They will also receive an internship in a targeted diocesan school that will offer a placement of excellence; targeted professional learning and unique on the job experience in schools and the central office, with a number of priority interviews for employment in schools on completion of studies, and with guaranteed employment. They will also be guaranteed a placement within a CEDWW school on completion of studies as well as support, and given advice with regard to Accreditation to Work, Teach and Lead.

It is heartening to see the ACU is offering to add 5 ATAR marks to those Year 11 and 12 students who undertake the ACU Youth Academy programme which combines features of youth ministry under the auspices of the Catholic Youth Ministry International (Australia) umbrella. This is a formal accreditation and the bonus marks help towards degree entry at the ACU. In a partnership between the ACU and Brisbane Catholic Education, pre-service teachers are undertaking the Spiritual and Pedagogical accompaniment (SPA) program which upon recent review (media release 2/11/22) has shown an increase in Catholic literacy and feelings of connection and competency with these trainee teachers. Students in this program spend one day a week at a school for between 6–12 months, in addition to doing their placement there. This immersion experience and one-on-one mentoring with a designated companion build spiritual and pedagogical skills, and the confidence to take these into the classroom in their first employment in the profession and in the Catholic sector. There are plans to grow this program nationally, and internationally. The newly developed ACU Spiritus Program for leadership formation can be conducted as Professional Learning or as units of study in ACU courses. This enables practising teachers to reinvigorate their own witness and bring it back to the classroom fruitfully.

For students enrolled in teaching, the ACU began offering in 2022 a Formation for Ministry in Catholic Schools unit. The rationale for the unit notes that: *This unit aims to equip pre-service teachers and youth ministry Church leaders with the knowledge, skills, and expertise to develop Catholic schools and Church communities as dynamic expressions of evangelisation.* Another useful trajectory might be to offer those students who complete their course with a mark of 35 or above in Text and Traditions or Religions and Society Units 3/4, an acknowledgement of prior learning if they choose to do the Religious Education Certificate as an addition to their degree in teaching. These subjects are suffering a decline in numbers in Catholic schools, as are many Humanities subjects – History is almost history! So it will reward those who have already gained some understanding of the exegetical process, biblical context and the ongoing conversation that exists between religion and society in the public square.

So it appears that there is an increasing recognition and response to the urgency of need here. The sector needs both numbers and quality. One only has to look at the weekend advertisements in late August for the following year for senior RE positions and classroom RE teachers. We know that our enrolments in the sector are growing at the school level. Now we need to identify and target those potential students who may be thinking of a career in teaching and in teaching Religious Education. It is concerning when a classroom teacher in a Catholic primary school suggests she has learned most of her RE from watching *The Simpsons*!

Cultural immediacy is one thing, but our young teachers in these crucial primary years must know the gospel story from some immersion in the faith tradition, so that it can be passed on credibly at this profoundly formative stage. If we cannot ensure that the RE classroom teacher is an authentic witness, the instruction in that classroom may come out of a more reductive Christian Values approach. This may be *nice,* but lack of familiarity does not help embed the profound truth of the gospel narrative and its primacy in shaping a distinctly Catholic community.

We must also prioritise the young male student to build up masculine role models for children in schools. We need gender participation parity in the profession and a revalidation and respect for teaching as the means by which this country thrives. This is not the place for any lengthy discussion, but it is a reality that impacts all sectors. In our Catholic sector, the good thing is that we already have a ready-made appraisal of potential applicants that are past pupils, having watched them in the school context. We are in an inside position to know if the prospective scholarship pre-service teacher will be the authentic and committed witness the Catholic system needs. Having had the opportunity to mentor pre-service teachers when placed in a school for their practicum, it is pleasing to know that there are young teachers in training who will become excellent RE teachers, given the right support, welcome and feedback, as they grow their skills and confidence in the classroom.

We need to have teachers of authentic witness in the classroom so that their very spirit, as well as their curriculum content knowledge and pedagogical aptitude, is modelled in each and every lesson. It has been said *We teach who we are*, and that is absolutely essential in the RE class. We know our students can detect any sort of fakery or lack of expertise, and the classroom may become contested, rather than calm, when this happens. If we do not have well-credentialed witnesses as the learning leaders we are dishonouring the integrity of the subject and slighting the primacy of the Catholic faith as integral to the school's identity. These witnesses themselves sometimes need to be provocateurs questioning the cultural and moral relativism that can undermine revelation. Sometimes they need to critique the culture of the school and offer interventions and solutions that may help with reparation and healing. Sometimes, the perceptions teachers from other faculties hold about 'the RE teacher' need to be challenged and dismantled through generous and honest dialogue. Sometimes, the courage of reimagining this role is required too.

A witness in a Catholic school understands that their work is covenantal, rather than contractual. As recently as January 2022, the Vatican Congregation for Catholic Education released its latest Instruction, *The Identity of the Catholic School for a Culture of Dialogue*, which stated:

> In the Catholic school's educational project there is no separation between the time for learning and the time for formation, between acquiring notions and growing in wisdom. The various school subjects do not present only knowledge to be obtained, but also values to be acquired and truths to be discovered. All of which demands an atmosphere characterised by the search for truth in which competent, convinced and coherent educators – teachers of learning and

of life – may be a reflection, albeit imperfect but still vivid, of the one Teacher (Para 23).

Our model for all our teacherly exploits and endeavours is Jesus. We are therefore constantly reminded of his inclusionary ways, his gentleness with those who were marginalised or outcast, and his encouragement of those who exhibited faith (*Your faith has made you well*, Luke 17:19). We also know that Jesus questioned and critiqued the practice and behaviours of those who held religiously powerful positions, and who appointed humble followers who sometimes dithered and doubted. We know he taught through parables, engaging his listeners with the metaphors and images they understood; the Mustard Seed, the Lost Sheep, the Talents, the Good Soil, the Good Samaritan, The Loving Father (The Prodigal Son). Jesus knew how to pitch his content for understanding, appreciation and real life application. This was passed on through the disciples to later generations. All of it is participatory pedagogy, the original learning received and built-on through later application and action; the learning that becomes part of a continuum, a cherished tradition.

Today we find ourselves today passing on the faith narrative, refreshing it for a contemporary audience, true to tradition but responsive to the times in which we live. Sharkey (2015, p. 7) reminds us that we need to 'draw deeply from our cultural myths to tell new stories that make sense for new times'. As has been frequently observed, it is through storytelling that values, ideas and customs are passed on and reshaped in new iterations that align with community expectations and understandings. The RE teacher as authentic storyteller and witness is crucial if the Catholic project is to continue to grow alongside the secular impulse and usefully critique those norms, behaviours and attitudes that do not dignify what it is to be human. As Bernadette and I can attest, we have long told the stories of our tradition and various congregational founders whilst managing to refresh the original narrative with contemporary parlance and understanding.

We know of Jesus' radical hospitality and his counter-cultural and provocative encounters with the religious elders of his own time. There are times when we as witnesses also need to be counter-cultural. This means we speak up and are counted when necessary; that we take daily prophetic action in our classrooms to tell the truth; that we plant seeds that supplant old ideas and practices; that we regenerate what it is to live as witnesses to our faith. This is where our next generation of RE teachers may be well-positioned, in tune as they are with the zeitgeist, but with the discernment that comes from understanding their own faith tradition.

The creation of a coercive class climate is antithetical to any generative learning experience that we would hope are our students' experiences. The search for truth must be invitational, dialogic and purposeful. As such, the personal disposition of the teacher is important as they relate to the organic nature of the classroom. It is imperative that the RE teacher is aware of the mood of the room, and has a broad understanding of Fowler's *Stages of Faith* and how these may be enacted in the attitude of students. External events may impact the class, such as exam pressures or other public concerns, and the good RE teacher knows how to deal with this in the most optimal and professional manner for all. It may mean some quick thinking in the way of modification of the lesson (or sequence of lessons).

As we know from the experience of the Covid 19 pandemic, external forces can impact best practice in the classroom and sometimes the RE teacher's response must be personal and gentle. Exceptions and accommodations may need to be made. This may well be the lesson recalled later; not the facts or dates or places, but the feelings that were responded to pastorally. This is a lesson in compassion and consideration, placing the child at the centre of their learning and life situation, responding in a way that is realistic and helpful. This is the witness that is strong enough to accommodate occasional interruptions that may impact scope and sequence and planned classroom learning. This is the witness of compassion modelled by Jesus.

Our second recommendation is that schools abandon the common practice of using RE as a filler to top up teachers' loads. In practice, this means in a Catholic school that an English or Humanities teacher can have a class of RE added to complete their load. They may be happy enough to teach it but may have limited faith background or requisite skills. Teaching out of field (Hobbs et al., 2021) may not enhance the learning experience for the student and this is not an authentic fit if we want to seriously develop the subject. We do a disservice, both to the subject and the students, if we do not prioritise the capacity and agency of those who teach it, as we would in core subjects. The other consideration to be made, in the light of the busyness of the secondary school and the occasional uphill battle for attention in some RE classes, is that a person not be overloaded with RE. A judicious balancing of the teacher's load is important and very few teachers would want a total RE teaching allocation. Care must be taken that an RE teacher never feels residualised or that they have been 'dumped' with or into classes. This is not good for morale or for the innovative freshness or energy needed to bring the subject alive.

We acknowledge the occasional resistance and disregard shown towards RE by some students – teachers need to choreograph lessons that are as inviting as possible, whilst not diluting content or making it all about entertainment. That right balance needs to be struck. As with most teacher-student interactions, the relational component is crucial in creating a congenial learning environment. A trusting and authentic teacher-student relationship in the classroom can become the ignition for engagement and effort. Humour does not hurt either! Again, our younger teachers will also have the language of connection, and the vernacular of youth, with which to engage their classes, knowing the right entry point for opening up new topics.

Our experience is that, despite its centrality to the identity of the school, RE can be sacrificed to the exigencies of the timetable. This dispensability may be diminishing as the ECSIP influence takes seed, but care still needs to be taken so that RE is not subsumed into a health/wellbeing/values conglomerate. Leadership of the school also needs to overtly value the subject. We do not need to hear from anyone, especially at a senior level, that 'It's only RE'. This is disparaging to both the subject and the teacher, not to mention the school's faith-based cornerstone of education. It comes down to appointments at an executive level who are also Catholic, or who understand, respect and support the ethos and culture of the school. As Horner (2021) makes clear, formation and the way we act 'theologically' every day can have a great impact on the reality of the Catholic identity of the school (p.7).

Horner (2021) contends that although some consider theology arcane and irrelevant, everyone in a Catholic school is always and already doing theology, whether they are aware of this or not, and whether they do it well or badly. This is accomplished in four different ways:

a. The teacher who has given up on the institutional Church because of its chauvinism or its clericalism or because of the crimes of sexual abuse, has made a theological decision, and communicates this, even if indirectly
b. The teacher who models a lack of engagement in liturgy has made a theological decision and communicates this to students perhaps more obviously than he or she is aware
c. The teacher who is critical of those who are living in same-sex relationships has made a theological decision and sometimes

communicates this without thought for care of the people involved, or onlookers

d. The teacher who is opposed to religion but likes working in a Catholic school has made a theological decision, and often communicates this with a kind of cynicism.

As Horner explains, this list could go on, but at its core is the fact that respect for Catholic identity and its visible enactment is required by all staff. We have been present at liturgies where staff behaviour has been casual, if not irreverent, and this is what the students see. The School Eucharist is not the time for a curriculum discussion in the back row or the specifics of weekend plans! Modelling is powerful. Actions do speak louder than words. Naturally, we would be very respectful if we entered a mosque, synagogue, temple, shrine or other place of worship. This same respect needs to be exercised in the liturgical practice of our home tradition. A casual treatment of the Catholic identity of a school can only weaken it, so we need to hire people who have a predisposition to the Christian worldview or who can happily align with the institutional behaviours and expectations of the school.

This also has legal implications about the hiring practices in Catholic and other faith-based schools so that these schools can continue to operate according to their beliefs and practices. This contentious issue is currently being debated in the Religious Discrimination Bill and the Inquiry into the Framework of Religious Exemptions in Anti-Discrimination Legislation. This is to ensure a fair and reasonable balance with other protected rights and this must be done with keen oversight and sensitivity to matters of suitability and personhood.

However, as noted in *The Identity of the Catholic School for a Culture of Dialogue* (2022) 'the predominant presence of a group of Catholic teachers can ensure the successful implementation of the educational plan developed in keeping with the Catholic identity of the schools' (Para 47). This is written forty years after the prescient words of *Lay Catholics in Schools* (1982) which stated: 'For it is the lay teachers, and indeed all lay persons, believers or not, who will substantially determine whether or not a school realizes its aims and accomplishes its objectives' (Para 2).

It would appear that last century there was an early recognition that other-than-believers and non-believers would be part of the Catholic education project. Teachers' contribution to the strengthening or diminishing of Catholic identity in their public attitudes and behaviour, particularly at school, is crucial. The diversity of the staff demographic is a microcosm of the world beyond the school and reflects the currents and changes in the secular world. We must work where we are and with those who are employed in this sector. This is not about conversion or control, but simply about mutuality and respect for those whose worldview is Christian.

In relation to lay educators in Catholic schools, it is important to distinguish between professionalism and vocation. Naturally professionalism is an integral aspect of this responsibility in shaping the hearts and minds of the young. However, with the ministry and mission of educating in faith, the recent Instruction states: 'The life of the Catholic teacher must be marked by the exercise of a personal vocation in the Church, and not simply by the exercise of a profession' (*Culture of Dialogue*, 2022, Para 24). Thus a demonstrable affiliation with the Church and its teachings, and a witness to this, is combined with a teacher's professional expertise.

The work of the Catholic teacher is to help form human beings, to bring them to a wholeness of self in all its dimensions. This goes far beyond the transmission of facts and theories, concepts and conjunctions, tick-box assessments or text response essays. Catholic teachers are in the business of soul work – '… for the teacher does not write on inanimate material but on the very spirit of human beings.'

(*Lay Catholics in Schools*, 1982, Para 19). What a magnificent thought and what a responsibility this is to handle all those students in front of us who are seeking to find their rightful place in the world and to make their unique contribution to the human story. Elsewhere, Ann, in a somewhat fulsome definition of what she does each day, has written that she does not simply teach, rather she works for eternity! That's what might be called a definition for the lay teacher privileged to work in the Catholic school as part of the Church's evangelising mission.

## Specialist

Related to the idea of Witness is that of RE teachers being Specialists in their field. With many of these teachers coming from Catholic backgrounds that may have only included being a student in a Catholic school themselves, the importance of providing opportunities for them to further their understanding of scripture, theology and Religious Education cannot be underestimated. In secondary schools, unlike teachers of Science or English, for example, RE teachers have not usually majored in this subject in their degree, with only some having completed a diploma or masters of education that included an RE element. This in itself is the reason to give RE teachers further opportunities to build and extend their knowledge so they are as well qualified as teachers in other subject areas. As Sharkey (2019) reminds us, our students in Catholic schools need to be taught by teachers who both know and love the faith.

Professional learning for RE teachers can take a variety of forms. Dowling (2012) emphasises that effective professional learning for RE educators should be grounded within a range of principles, processes, structures and activities that have as their focus the development of the knowledge, values, relationships and practices that have a positive impact on the learning outcomes of religious education students (p. 28). Whilst it is valuable to send RE teachers to conferences and

Figure 9.2: In Moscow and Ravenna Italy with parish friends.

seminars, fuller, more ongoing forms of professional learning, such as full subjects at a suitable religious university or college, or diplomas or bachelor degrees, can often have more enduring benefits for the teacher and his/her students.

As mentioned in the previous chapter, part of the role of the Religious Education Coordinator is to oversee the professional learning of their team of teachers and provide opportunities for them to engage in it. In reality, it may be difficult for schools to free teachers to attend external professional learning, but this should be considered a priority in a Catholic school. We recommend that scholarships be provided by schools, parent groups and Catholic Education offices for teachers to do more extended study such as a Bachelor or Master of Theology or Religious Education. (Ann was a fortunate recipient here in being able to undertake a Masters in Educational Leadership at the ACU at 25 per cent of the normal cost for such a course.)

Another area that could usefully inform and enthuse the RE teacher is subsidised travel to the Holy Land. This may take the form of a pilgrimage, sabbatical, further study or part of a unit at university. Imagine, then, how this could rejuvenate the reality of the classroom teaching experience when teachers could speak with authority on the life and times of Jesus of Nazareth, having walked in his footsteps, prayed where he prayed and gained a deeper appreciation of the profound impact of the Judeo-Christian story on the development of Western civilisation. Bernadette has experienced this with her parish community and would highly recommend it. Such an immersive experience would be both personally and professionally beneficial for the RE teachers, and this would flow on into the classroom as enriched learning for the students.

Many religious orders today offer their RE staff study tours or pilgrimages to places central to their founding story or charism. With enriched knowledge and insight, the teacher can speak confidently about the spiritual motivations of the founder in their life and times and refresh it for today's telling. With the diminution in vocations worldwide, the charism of many orders will be carried on by lay people who have undertaken special formation by way of accompaniment or lay apostolate. Having been privileged to go on two such pilgrimages with the FCJ and Dominican sisters, Ann can say that these have been facilitative in discerning the animating spirit of the religious congregation and bringing this back to the classroom. Having completed formation as a Companion In Mission with the Faithful Companions of Jesus, Ann also knows just how important this is in a school and how these people can become a further resource with their more intimate connections with the order.

It is understood that leadership teams, governance and board members often undertake these journeys so that they have an appreciation of the school's abiding ethos. They may do a staff presentation on return, but how is that percolating down to the student cohort? Leadership moves on but more often than not the classroom teacher is a stayer. It is this classroom teacher who needs first-hand knowledge to convey the power and primacy of faith stories. It is this classroom teacher who is the daily, lesson by lesson, on-the-ground expert. It is their witness, not the odd word from the principal at an assembly, that effectively sows the seeds for future faith. As Rymarz and Sharkey (2019) observe, 'It is in the classroom setting that the human encounter that is at the heart of the gospel takes place' (p. 2).

Another area that needs attention is the formation of senior or executive staff. Much as these educators may, or may not, have a Catholic background, they, too, need depthing in the particular spirituality or charism of the school they work for. This needs to be more than a couple of days' induction and some biographical notes about the founder. Schools are busy places and new staff need to jump in with energy and adapt to the culture of the school and its particular systems. However, if the Catholic identity of the school is to be fruitfully bolstered there needs to be 'an expectation that teachers and leaders cultivate and embody Gospel-based beliefs, values and witness' (Gowdie, 2017, p. 20). The diminution of Catholic identity comes from the top. The principal may be a fervent witness to faith, but they also need a leadership team around them that exercises this visibly. This is the embodiment that needs to be seen and internalised by students, a leadership density prioritising the faith. When school leaders become confident in this area their whole referencing system can naturally allude to a founding story, anecdote or impulse, without this feeling like an awkward add-on.

Gowdie (2017) goes on to remark that spiritual formation is the 'sleeping giant' for Catholic education and can fall into the soft edge of professional development, and thereby not be seen as important as other professional learning. However, for her, and for us, this is probably the most crucial area of concern. She writes, 'The creation of a contemporary approach to spiritual formation that is both faithful to the evangelising mission of the Church, and responsive to the personal worlds of individuals, calls us to be creative and practical, to reimagine traditional approaches, and to recover core realities' (Gowdie, 2017, p. 23). If our students are to reap the multiple blessings of a Catholic education, the collective staff soul needs to be visibly in sync with the mission of the school. This is even more important for those in positions of leadership which may have a more public or communal role. As a challenge this will require time, grounding, ongoing effort and generous mutuality between staff and system. Such deep formation is imperative for the health and growth of our educational project in what we can offer our students as they come to know themselves as spiritual beings, active agents, and their own best selves.

## Moderator

This is the final aspect of being an RE teacher according to Pollefeyt (2008) and can be seen in the more familiar terms of moving from being 'a sage on the stage to a guide on side.' However, being a guide or facilitator is not as simple as it may sound. In fact, it is a more skilful role than being a guru up front. From a secular perspective, a skilled moderator needs to be one who 'orchestrates the context, provides the resources, and poses questions to stimulate students to think up their own answers' (King, 1998, p. 30).

Within the hermeneutical context of a RE classroom, a moderator is called to guide students through the 'complex and multifaceted correlations between their own experiences and religious and non-religious traditions' (Pollefeyt, 2008, p. 15). This aligns with the Pedagogy of Encounter that we referred to in earlier chapters as this encourages students to respond to a provocation in terms of how they and others might encounter this, the implications for others, the world and God, and how the Catholic Church might respond to it. They are then called to commitment and action. This is not necessarily an easy process for all teachers to navigate and begs the question as to how we effectively support them in doing so. Our recommendation is to mentor collaborative groups for RE teachers.

In order to be effective moderators in the cut and thrust of the RE classroom, the first place to start is within the school's RE team. In this team there will be individual worldviews and predispositions, biases and concerns, pedagogical variations and preferences. However, the connectivity and respect within the group is already established through its members' strong identification and affiliation with the Catholic faith and their desire to pass this on to their students. Collaboration is almost a given in this group where goodwill is often the keynote of endeavours, both within the delivery of curriculum and in the active faith life of the school.

However, in many schools these teams are chasing their tails trying to find time to meet at irregular after-school times or lunchtimes. Over the years, Ann has attended any number of 7.45 am meetings, rushing off to yard or tram duty at 8.10! Such necessarily rushed gatherings of team members are not conducive to genuine discussions about what might be helpful strategies to engage different cohorts of students, or to unpack the ways of using the Pedagogy of Encounter in different contexts. Hence our recommendation is that schools give priority for RE teams to have timetabled meetings where there is an emphasis on planning and delivery. Although some teachers might find this burdensome initially, being able to step into their classrooms with increased confidence and having a supportive community to return to share their successes and failures cannot be underestimated. This is what Wenger and Wenger (2020) call 'learning loops'. These learning loops help everyone to continually improve their teaching:

> When someone hears what another participant has done they may be inspired to try something similar. Or they may be warned against trying it if it didn't work … this systemises the learning by spreading it among members (Wenger-Trayner et al., 2020, p. 132).

As such, this revised learning and sharing of approaches and material amongst RE staff teaching similar things assists in moderation. This is because there is a constantly renewed and responsive insight and understanding. A moderator is, among many things, also a life-long learner.

A moderator has to look at the teaching and learning agenda to find ways that will provide access to meaning for all in the class. This requires sensitivity and discernment and, especially in today's climate, a grasp of the cultural underground of our students and the rapid rate of change occasioned by digital innovation and new technologies. A moderator must be apprised of the world beyond the Catholic lens, even though that lens is necessarily favoured and preferred by the school. They will need to understand the inherent dignity of each class member and their unique journey to realised selfhood. Consequently, the classroom becomes a place of freedom and safety where a student can articulate their position or thinking in a supportive environment. However, this journey to maturity is no longer simple. We live in a world where technology can make or break a student's sense of self and their personal agency. Our children live in a world of distractions and addictions, cyber-bullying, sleep deprivation, exposure to sexualised content, and constantly shifting social mores curated by Tik-Tok and SnapChat. It is a world that is open 24/7 where parents and teachers can no longer put locks on doors to keep children safe. As Lenehan (2017) notes, the moderator 'creates genuine encounters of dialogue that respect particularity and alterity among diverse faith stances and worldviews' (p. 153). The moderator is aware of a world that tempts, and which contests attitudes, norms and values. The moderator aims to mediate these justly and authoritatively to discharge the care and responsibility they owe all those in their classroom.

Our job is to educate our students thoughtfully so that they can navigate this changing world and make good decisions for themselves and others. Moderators need the capacity to discern what is true, beautiful and good and what is cheap and nasty. They may offer an alternative template for action and behaviour. They may well be the actual moderator in a robust and contentious in-class debate where heightened emotions can run rampant because these are topics that create passion or outrage. This is where the moderator's flexibility, finesse and common sense come into play. It is also a place where all voices are heard courteously and the notion of civil public conversation is modelled. The REC, too, may on the odd occasion have to moderate discussion within the staff group on a topic when there are opposing views as to how it should be presented to students. It is not always about finding a middle path, but the right path for the circumstances and those involved in it. Moderators should be able to capably practise the Pedagogy of Encounter both in the staffroom and the classroom where a convergence of ideas and actions may fruitfully take place.

## References

Boeve L, 'Religious education in a post-secular and post-Christian,' *Journal of Beliefs & Values*, 33:2, 2012, pp. 143-156, doi.10.1080/13617672.2012.694058

Boeve L, 'Horizon: The challenge of plurality and difference,' in Boeve, *Theology at the crossroads of university, church and society : dialogue, difference and Catholic identity*, pp. 33-53, Bloomsbury T&T Clark, 2016.

Dowling E, 'An investment in our future: Reimagining professional learning for religious educators', *Journal of Religious Education*, 2012.

Gowdie J, *Stirring the Soul of Catholic Education*, Vaughan Publishing, Melbourne, 2017

Hobbs L and Porsch R, 'Teaching out-of-field: challenges for teacher education', *European Journal of Teacher Education*, 44:5, pp. 601-610, 2021, doi: 10.1080/02619768.2021.1985280

Hobbs L & Porsch R, 'Teaching out-of-field: challenges for teacher education', *European Journal of Teacher Education*, 44:5, pp. 601-610, 2021, doi: 10.1080/02619768.2021.1985280

Horner, R, 'Enhancing Catholic School Identity through Religious Education', Conference paper, Australian Catholic University, 2020.

King A, 'Sage on the Stage to Guide on the Side', *College Teaching*, 41:1, pp. 30-35 Taylor & Francis, 1993, http://www.jstor.org/stable/27558571 Accessed: 24/5/2022

Lay Catholics in Schools: Witnesses to Faith, Congregation for Catholic Education, 15/10/82

Lenehan K, 'RE Curriculum Renewal in Victorian Catholic Schools', *Moving from Theory to Practice*, Vaughan Publishing, Melbourne, 2017.

Pollefeyt D, 'Difference Matters. A Hermeneutic-Communicative Concept of Didactics of Religion in a European, Multi-Religious Context', *Journal of Religious Education*, 56 (1), Australian Catholic University, 2008.

Rymarz R & Sharkey P, *Moving from Theory to Practice*, Vaughan Publishing, Melbourne, 2019.

The Identity of the Catholic School for a Culture of Dialogue, Congregation for Catholic Education, 25/1/2022.

Sharkey P, *Catholic Identity*, Garratt Publishing, Melbourne, 2015.

Wenger-Trayner E & Wenger-Trayner B, *Learning to Make a Difference: Value Creation in Social Learning Spaces*, Cambridge University Press, doi: 10.1017/9781108677431

## Reflection

1. What programmes and innovations would help provide a steady flow of committed younger teachers to the RE classroom?
2. How is the 'energy' of the RE staff at your school?
3. What professional learning would enhance the quality and confidence of prospective RE teachers?
4. Can you identify a need or any gaps in the formation of leaders in your school?

# CHAPTER ELEVEN
## Summary

Teaching Religious Education in our time is clearly not for the faint-hearted. Yet we can both profess that when it goes well, there is no better subject to teach. We love engaging with students around the deep questions of life and helping them to understand ancient scriptural texts and see relevance for them in their own lives. We marvel at the capacity of students to engage in meditation and other forms of reflection and their passion and activism for issues such as refugees, climate change, environmental sustainability, poverty and gender equality. We admire their sense of justice and inclusion and the demand that the world should be a place where discrimination, stigma and bias are things of the past. We know that they have dreams and energy, just as we did. We also know that they need wise heads to guide them as they recreate a world prioritised by the common good.

For this book, we have used as our title and the chapter overviews the *witness, specialist, moderator* concept that has come out of the Enhancing Catholic School Identity Project emanating from Leuven University, Belgium. This framework means that we have referred to our own *witness* growing up in the Catholic faith and how this has shaped our own lives, identities and careers. *Specialist* delineates our post-graduate study, professional learning and ongoing interest and immersion in the vibrancy and viability of RE for teachers and students alike. The *moderator* suggests how we can be the conduit for topical and discerning engagement with the secular world in which we find ourselves, and how we can continue to bring the Good News to all in the contemporary Catholic classroom.

We have worked in contexts both local and international, variously explored committed religious life, engaged in theological and other study, travelled, married, parented and actively participated in our parish communities. We have committed ourselves to our profession and, importantly for this book, prioritised the teaching of religious education as part of our suite of pedagogical disciplines. We are now looking back to see where we have come from and to make some suggestions as to how the next generation of Catholic teachers might evangelise and enrich Catholic education in the light of its integral mission in the Church. We are alert to the need for sufficient numbers and suitable quality in the area of religious education as the older generation of 'rusted-on' RE teachers disappears and the primacy of the subject is contested. We are conscious of the recent words of Sharkey (2015):

> The Catholic school is an educational community where learning, culture and faith find a meeting place. The challenge of making this meeting place meaningful for students lies at the heart of the identity challenge faced by Catholic schools in our time. It is a challenge that is invigorating but demanding and becoming more sophisticated as each year unfolds (p. 1).

We note that there has been a discernible shift in the last three years as a consequence of the Covid 19 pandemic. This has impacted on the sense of connection and belonging of our young people in Catholic schools.

As has been noted in the recent Vatican document, *The Identity of a Catholic School for a Culture of Dialogue* (February 2022, para. 18) – 'The Catholic school lives in the flow of human history' and this is where we find ourselves today as we respond to the pervasive social, cultural and religious shifts which are changing the world and the way we inhabit it.

## Reflection

1. What global, national or local issues are engaging our youth today?
2. How can their activism contribute to the common good?
3. What further ideas do you have to propose a religious framework for thoughts and actions rather than simply altruism?
4. Today, learning, culture and faith find a meeting place in the Catholic school. What ideas/ innovations/ changes/ dreams do you have to make this encounter meaningful for students?

## CHAPTER TWELVE
## Concluding Thoughts

This book will be published as the implications of the 2021 census results begin to take shape. The results are predictable and concerning. For the first time since censuses began, there are fewer than 50 per cent of Australians identifying as Christian, whilst the numbers identifying as non-religious have soared from 30 per cent in 2016 to 39 per cent in 2021! As *The Sydney Morning Herald (28/6/2022)* reminds us, 'Australia has become strikingly more godless over the past decade.' In light of this, should we not be surprised that the students we are asked to teach have so little religious background and sometimes so little inclination to learn about a religion they have little connection with? We have watched as institutional authority has declined and personal ascendancy has replaced the communal impulse. No longer do we, even as committed Catholics, turn to our local parish priest in making moral decisions, or rush to attend a late Sunday evening Mass for fear of committing a mortal sin if we miss it.

~

As we look to the future of the Catholic school we are reminded that its duty is to constantly raise the God question. This can be done through respectful dialogue as the teacher speaks to the assorted class members about meaning, belief and values. And some of this may well be countercultural. In fact, being a bold minority in a secular society may clearly identify those who are adherents of the Catholic faith tradition. Is this not what the early Church was, a bold minority two millennia ago during the *Pax Romana*? The Catholic school may well be the place for formation and transformation of its students. For here they can engage in discourse both transcendent and temporal, moving them to a boldness that critiques and offers solutions to the climate of the times in a spirit of goodwill. Perhaps, in the work we teachers do day in day out, we need to act with an audacity of hope, animated and enlivened by the Holy Spirit.

Recently, in the *National Catholic Reporter* (4/5/2022) Daniel P Horan, a Franciscan priest, gives thoughtful consideration to the world inhabited by the young people we teach. He poses the question:

> *What if our starting point in thinking about what it means to be a person in communion with God, oneself and the world was not reduced to external expressions of institutional belonging, but instead began with attention to humans' inherent capacity for God? (p. 2)*

He refers to Ronald Rolheiser's description of spirituality: 'Long before we do anything religious at all, we have to do something about the fire that burns within us. What we do with that fire, how we channel it, is our spirituality' (*The Holy Longing: The Search for a Christian Spirituality*, 2009). We are in a privileged and responsible position, in the RE classroom and at the Catholic school, to help with that channelling, with that formative and purposeful finding for the student that they have a spiritual dimension, individually sparked and motivated, sometimes with a religious language and framework, sometimes without it, sometimes borrowing and reshaping it for today's lived reality.

Horan is optimistic about the future and suggests that the expression, 'I'm spiritual, but not religious' is not as threatening nor as bad as some in the institutional Church may fear. He thinks it may instead be a great sign of possibility and hope, provided there are avenues for leadership and accompaniment for the young who are

## Concluding Thoughts

seeking the spiritual and want to belong to a Church that empowers their faith and agency as they shape the institution for the 21st century. Respecting the tradition, they also want to refresh it for their times.

As *The Identity of the Catholic School for a Culture of Dialogue* makes clear, we must respond to the challenges of our times with the continuity of our faith tradition as we work in parallel with the growth of interreligious and intercultural dialogue (Paras 1 and 2) in a world that is increasingly secularised and pluralised. Mindful that we do not become defensive as we champion our tradition in the face of these contemporary challenges, Rossiter suggests that 'secular spirituality needs to be acknowledged and addressed in other than a deficit way' (Rossiter, 2017, p. 29). Therefore, we need to look outwards in new directions, emboldened by the opportunity to guide and accompany our young people as they find the spirituality and meaning-making that converts into lives of purpose and service.

We recognise how vastly the world has changed in the last five decades and that we need new 'tellings' and appropriations of our long-held narratives. We cannot continue as we were and must adapt, spiritually and strategically, to continue to tell the salvation story of Jesus of Nazareth – to make it known and meaningful for a contemporary audience. Our Christian story is two thousand years and forever old, and has been retold and refreshed over time and place. It must be again if it is to tell its abundant and glorious truth two millennia from now.

As teachers in the Catholic education system in Australia, we need to ask the same question as the Plenary Council 2022 is asking: What is the Holy Spirit asking of us at this time? The aim of the Plenary Council is to renew the life and mission of the Church in Australia. This process needs listening and discernment and implementation through thoughtful, collaborative action with a unity of intention. The hope is that new growth from the Plenary will impact our education system in ways that open up communion and regenerate what we do in ways that honour the past, speak to the present and look to the future. Bernadette and I have attempted to provide some answers that may assist in looking ahead hopefully as we continue with the project that is Catholic education in this wide brown land we, along with First Nations custodians and newer settlers, call home.

We know that the Christ story is front and centre and that we are contemporary disciples sent forth on a distinctive mission. We know we need the next generation of committed Catholic teachers to be able to dialogue gently and respectfully with a changing world, holding onto the deep anchor of faith in sometimes turbulent waters. We know that these teachers will often be the most influential religious educators for the child, in response to parents outsourcing this aspect of their upbringing for almost as long as we have been teaching.

We are reminded in the words of Saint John Henry Newman:

*God has created me to do Him some definite service. He has committed some work to me which He has not committed to another. I have my mission. I may never know it in this life, but I shall be told it in the next … I am a link in a chain, a bond of connection between persons. He has not created me for naught. I shall do good; I shall do His work. I shall be an angel of peace, a preacher of truth in my own place…* (Meditations on Christian Doctrine, Hope in God, Para 2, March 7, 1848).

Each of us finds our own place where we can do good. For the RE teacher that is in the classroom mostly, but also on retreat, when meditating with students, during Mass or other liturgical celebrations, when praying, when planning collaboratively with other teachers to ensure that the material and its delivery finds an entry point and the necessary engagement of those in the class. Sometimes all this happens in the incidental interactions of the corridor or playground or house meetings, in the cheerful greeting exchanged and the personal interest shown in a student. Michael Green suggests '… it is for all of us to lift our heads out of the figurative scrums that the freneticism of school life can induce and to be in awe of what is at play. God is seeking revelation and the life of God is seeking expression' ( Green, 2018, p. 23). As we go about our work, we must look to see God in all things, in the ebb and flow of school life swirling all around us, in the core realities of our daily lives.

Pope Francis, too, speaks of mission:

*I am on a mission on this earth; that is why I am here in the world. We have to regard ourselves as sealed, even branded by this mission of bringing light, blessing, enlivening, raising up, healing and freeing. All around us we begin to see nurses with soul, teachers with soul, politicians with soul, people who have chosen deep down to be with others and for others* (Pope Francis, *Evangelii Gaudium* notes, 2013, pp. 133-134 & 273).

The pontiff is speaking directly to all of those who are in Catholic education. We are teachers with soul and know of so many others who have undertaken this fraternal soul-work in the course of their professional careers and their ministry of witness. We are links in the chain of the Catholic continuum, doing our bit, staying the course. Perhaps all those committed RE teachers can look to the words of 2 Timothy 4:7 as something of an epitaph for their lives and careers and take comfort in the words: *I have fought the good fight; I have finished the race; I have kept the faith.*

Bernadette and I may be in the last few years of our RE teaching mission in schools, but we care that our work goes forward; better, brighter, realisable and influential for a new generation. As we pass the baton on, we are reminded of those words from Jeremiah 29:11. 'For I know the plans I have for you,' declares the LORD, 'plans to prosper you and not to harm you, plans to give you hope and a future.' So it is important that we plan ahead for the project of Catholic education, imagining possibilities, charting new territory, being provoked and challenged by the world around us and finding our place, perhaps as that bold minority to which Greg Sheridan referred. We must be motivated to do what we can, where we can. This book is motivated by our desire to do that bit more in our sphere in the hope that it opens conversations that will enlarge and ennoble what we do as RE teachers on a daily basis.

We also know that serious conversations need to be had within the local and national leadership, both clerical and educational, to recognise the gravity of the situation and the urgent need to invite, train, professionalise and support the next generation of RE teachers.

Catholic writer and thinker G K Chesterton stated that 'Education is simply the soul of a society as it passes from one generation to another' (GK Chesterton, as reported in the Observer Newspaper, 1924). Perhaps, when we speak of the Religious Education of the next generation this is ever more so the case, particularly as we invite students into the Christian cosmology that is underwritten by forgiveness, redemption and eternal hope. Pierre Teilhard de Chardin SJ, philosopher and palaeontologist, reminded us that we are not 'human beings having a spiritual experience, but spiritual beings having a human experience.' We are mindful of those currently or soon to be in our classrooms, boys and girls – spiritual beings – who will be taught by the next generation of teachers. We see these teachers as being a bridge between our faith tradition and the culture the students find themselves in. This dynamic exchange of dialogue involving both faith and culture will be a relevant entry point for our future students.

## Concluding Thoughts

Teachers, both in RE and in other disciplines in the Catholic system, will have at their fingertips the promise of evangelical opportunity in whatever shape that takes. As Gowdie (2017) notes, 'the possibilities for genuine transformative work that changes lives and influences the world has never been so verdant!' (p. 22). Perhaps we should be aiming to lift the Spirit for all our young people. The blessing of the RE classroom is that we can be at the frontline of addressing what Pope Francis calls the 'globalisation of indifference' (8/7/2013, Homily, 'Arena' Sports Camp, Salina Quarter, Lampedusa). This is enacted in the way we open up the world and invite our students to respond to others, such as their neighbours near and far, with compassion, empathy, solidarity and justice.

Our students – we believe – will be provided with a solid guiding framework for navigating a complex and confusing world with its myriad messages, influences and attractions. Perhaps they will live out that 'revolution of tenderness' (*Evangelli Gaudium* n. 88) of which the pontiff also speaks.

Our next generation of RE teachers can be thought-leaders and influencers, way beyond the ephemerality of the TikTok meme or being Insta-famous. They can influence, form and transform the child in front of them by holding onto our foundational convictions and responding with hope and discernment in the light of the secular pluralist world we now live in. We truly hope that the joys and mystery of the Catholic imagination and what it stands for is rekindled for the next generation of the faithful. Bernadette and I learned in our own Catholic education the primacy of loving God and loving neighbour. That lesson remains absolute and inviolate. However, it may well be delivered very differently today in response to a world that has changed irrevocably. Our young people today have different inputs and outputs and we must respond to those authentically. We need new ways to assist in their best *becoming* if we are to balance change and tradition in a world whose certainties are less sure than they once were. Our hope and prayer is that this mediated lesson of an integrated living between faith and culture takes seed and blossoms in the hearts and minds, actions and behaviours of the generations who come after us.

Paul Kelly writing in *The Australian* just after the 2021 census results were released, notes, 'The long historical view suggests the great religions possess immense recuperative power and Christianity has an underestimated institutional influence in Australia with the potential for revival' (*The Weekend Australian*, 2–3 July 2022, p 15). These are encouraging words that can breathe new life into our endeavours as we, with our students, identify what David Tacey calls 'the new locations of the sacred' (2000, p. 235). We may have a renewal, a renaissance, a resurgence when it is discovered that we really do need the strong moral structures and the cohering social values of our Judeo-Christian heritage that have brought us thus far. We have two thousand years of our enduring faith tradition behind us and a future story to which to contribute. We are on a threshold of transition to the writing of new chapters in new ways.

This has been evidenced concretely by Pope Francis who has recently made an apostolic journey to Canada for the first time and has apologised for the treatment of Indigenous people in Church-based institutions. He knows that the Church is a fallible institution because it is populated by human beings – Us. We know where we have failed, institutionally and personally, but we also believe in forgiveness and redemption. In his Vespers Homily of the July 28 2022, the pontiff has made distinct reference to the challenge of secularisation. In doing so he asks that we not look back nostalgically to the glory days of the Church and rue the past, but that we look forward with joy as we discern how we can build the Kingdom better.

We finish writing this book just as Pope Francis celebrates the 60th anniversary of the opening of Vatican II on 11 October 1962.

## Concluding Thoughts

As we have noted, the world is in a different place and the role of institutional religion in the public square is increasingly contested. This has recently been seen in a number of situations locally where the primacy of corporate values that support inclusivity and diversity have militated against a person of faith holding a public role, or private views, that may not be popularly supported. Some have noted that this is simply the Christian, Jewish and Muslim faith traditions holding fast to their traditional, formative and often conservative values in the face of progress.

Religious freedom to publicly express faith and its traditional tenets is seen, in some circles, to not align with a secular values charter. There is increasing pressure for groups and corporations to adopt mission and vision statements prioritising these secular or 'citizen' values. For some, this may well create a tension between their private faith stance and their public role. Christopher Middleton SJ (*Eureka Street*, 10 October, 2022) notes that there is a widespread perception that Christian viewpoints are being excluded from the public square. Frank Brennan SJ argues that we need to 'advocate without accusation, disagree without disrespect and see differences as places of encounter, rather than exclusion' (*The Weekend Australian*, 8/9 October 2022). Pope Francis in his homily on the anniversary of Vatican II reminded us to 'look around'. In other words, being in the world with others without ever feeling superior to others, and being servants of that higher realm which is the Kingdom of God (cf. *Lumen Gentium*, 5); bringing the good news of the Gospel into people's lives and languages (cf. *Sacrosanctum Concilium*, 36), sharing their joys and hopes (cf. *Gaudium et Spes*, 1).

In his address to the World Union of Catholic Teachers (11 Dec 2022) Pope Francis reiterates the importance of renewal of mission and again asserts that the presence of Christian educators in the school world is of vital importance. He stated:

*The style he or she assumes is decisive. In fact, the Christian educator is called to be fully human and fully Christian at the same time. There is no humanism without Christianity. And there is no Christianity without humanism.*

The pontiff warns against any rigidity of approach and reminds Catholic teachers that whilst they adopt and adapt language and cultural forms to reach the young, they must also guard against ideological colonisation. Teachers must continue to discern the difference between the novelty that enables growth and flourishing and an ideology that can cause enduring harm. It is important, he added, that Catholic teachers be capable of testifying that the Christian faith embraces all of human experience, 'without clipping the wings of young peoples' dreams and impoverishing their aspirations'. He refers to the art of education. All teachers know that part of this art is the fine balance struck when we know who we are teaching, how and why and where it may yet take our young people as they build their futures, individually and collectively.

So, as we forge ahead, it may well be that secularisation has impacted to such an extent that to publicly avow faith is seen as oppositional to a more secular worldview. This may yet have implications for Catholic schools, their selection of employees in the light of equality and/or discrimination, and how to creatively and committedly energise the faith for the betterment of all in a time when faith is disparaged or seen as irrelevant and anachronistic. These elements go to the heart of Catholic identity.

We need to find places of reconciliation when irreconcilable differences threaten to divide us. We need to find those mutual meeting places as we mould and form the next generation of Catholics and those young people of goodwill, of no faith or other faith traditions, who companion us in different ways. We are reminded that our schools are schools for all and that 'Catholic identity is a place of encounter, a tool for promoting the convergence of ideas and actions' (*The Identity of a Catholic School for a Culture of Dialogue*, para 84, February 2022). These ideas and actions build the common good and unify the human family, a responsive and generative outgrowth from the transcendent truth that inspires us.

We have challenging times ahead in our Catholic education sector. However, we live in hope that a new generation of teachers, and most especially the Religious Education teacher, will be able to exercise their own authentic *witness, specialist, moderator* experience for the flourishing of all in the contemporary Catholic classroom.

We have great faith in this educational enterprise. It is vital to the mission of the Church and to the holistic, humanising and spiritual growth of all the young people we are privileged to teach in this Great South Land of the Holy Spirit.

## References

Boeve L, 'Religious education in a post-secular and post-Christian,' *Journal of Beliefs & Values*, 33:2, 2012, pp. 143-156, doi.10.1080/13617672.2012.694058

Boeve L, 'Horizon: The challenge of plurality and difference', in Boeve, *Theology at the crossroads of university, church and society : dialogue, difference and Catholic identity*, pp. 33-53, Bloomsbury T&T Clark, 2016.

Dowling E, 'An investment in our future: Reimagining professional learning for religious educators', *Journal of Religious Education*, 2012.

Green M, *Now with Enthusiasm: Charism, God's mission and Catholic Schools Today*, Garratt Publishing, 2018.

Gowdie J, *Stirring the Soul of Catholic Education*, Vaughan Publishing, Melbourne, 2017.

Hobbs L and Porsch R, 'Teaching out-of-field: challenges for teacher education', *European Journal of Teacher Education*, 44:5, pp. 601-610, 2021, doi: 10.1080/02619768.2021.1985280

Horan, D, *National Catholic Reporter*, 4/5/22 Newman J H, 'A Short Visit to the Blessed Sacrament before Meditation, Part 111', *Meditations on*

*Christian Doctrine, Hope in God*, March 7, 1848.

King A, 'Sage on the Stage to Guide on the Side', *College Teaching*, *41*:1, pp. 30-35 Taylor & Francis, 1993, http://www.jstor.org/stable/27558571 Accessed: 24/5/2022

Lenehan K, 'RE Curriculum Renewal in Victorian Catholic Schools', *Moving from Theory to Practice*, Vaughan Publishing, 2017.

Newman J H, 'A Short Visit to the Blessed Sacrament before Meditation, Part 111', *Meditations on Christian Doctrine, Hope in God*, March 7, 1848.

Pollefeyt D, 'Difference Matters. A Hermeneutic-Communicative Concept of Didactics of Religion in a European, Multi-Religious Context', *Journal of Religious Education, 56* (1), Australian Catholic University, 2008.

Pope Francis: Address at General Assembly of World Union of Catholic Teachers, Vatican, 11 December 2022.

Pope Francis: 60th Anniversary of the Beginning of the Second Vatican Ecumenical Council, Homily, St Peter's Basilica, 11 October 2022.

Pope Francis: Apostolic Exhortation, Evangelii Gaudium, On the Proclamation of the Gospel in Today's World, 24 November 2013.

Pope Francis: Apostolic Journey of His Holiness Pope Francis to Canada, 24-30 July, 2022, Homily, Basilica of Notre Dame de Quebec.

Rossiter G. 'A personal critical perspective on the development of Australian Catholics Schools' Religious education: Where to from here?', A. Belmonte and R. Rymarz, *Religious Education in Australian Catholic Schools: Exploring the Landscape*, Garratt Publishing, 2017.

Rymarz R and Sharkey P, *Moving from Theory to Practice*, Vaughan Publishing, Melbourne, 2019.

Sharkey P, *Catholic Identity*, Garratt Publishing, Melbourne, 2015.

Tacey, D, *Beyond Literal Belief*, Garratt Publishing, Melbourne, 2015.

Wenger-Trayner E and Wenger-Trayner B, *Learning to Make a Difference: Value Creation in Social Learning Spaces*, Cambridge University Press, doi: 10.1017/9781108677431 Wenger-Trayner E. & Wenger-Trayner B, *Learning to Make a Difference: Value Creation in Social Learning Spaces*, Cambridge University Press, doi: 10.1017/9781108677431

## Reflection

1. *We have to do something about the fire that burns within us* (Ronald Rolheiser). What fire is burning within you?
2. How do you see your distinctive mission as a disciple or teacher?
3. Can you find dynamic entry points between faith and culture to engage young people in their religious or spiritual journey?
4. What is helping you to balance change and tradition?
5. What challenges do you see ahead?
6. What hopes are lighting your way?

# Acknowledgements

The authors acknowledge the contributions from reviewers who played an essential role in reading our manuscript and sharing valuable comments. In particular, we thank Dr Rose-Marie Prosser, Ms. Margaret Waldeck and Dr Gavin Brown. These contributions were an essential ingredient necessary to improve our work.

We also thank the Genazzano Institute and its director, Ms Catherine Brandon, and Genazzano principal, Mrs Loretta Wholley, for supporting our work as a professional learning project. We would especially like to thank our colleagues and friends at both Genazzano FCJ College, Kew, and Our Lady of Mercy College, Heidelberg. Sometimes it was an incidental chat, words of encouragement, remarks made at an RE meeting, or a new insight shared that added richness or subtlety to what we wanted to say.

Thank you especially to Garratt Publishing who accepted our manuscript and provided the necessary processes to lead to final publication.

Finally, we dedicate this book to our families and to the valiant women of the Faithful Companions of Jesus and Loreto traditions whose influence on us was, and is, formative and profound.

*Dr Bernadette Mercieca*
Melbourne, Australia

*Ann Rennie*
Melbourne, Australia

# Appendix 1

### Example of Inquiry unit Year 9 RE at Xavier College

The basis for this inquiry unit at Year 9 is the *To Know Worship and Love* Chapter 3, The Catholic Church in Australia. Where previously a teacher would have worked through this chapter over a series of lessons, the following approach opens up the topic more broadly and allows students to direct their own learning.

### Step 1

The teacher presents a timeline of the story of the Catholic Church in Australia and over one or possibly two lessons gives an overview of the key events and figures.

### Step 2

Students work in small groups to brainstorm an 'unGoogleable' question related to a particular part of the timeline. On butcher's paper, they explore the aspects that they could consider in their research.

Possible topics could include:

- How and why was St Francis' Church built and what did it mean to people of that time?
- Why do we consider Mary MacKillop a saint?
- What were the implications of the Education Acts of 1872? Explain from two different perspectives.

The teacher ensures that a good variety of topics get chosen.

Step 3

Students spend 4–5 lessons researching their chosen topic and preparing a presentation.

Step 4

Each group presents their findings. The teacher adds more information if need be.

# Appendix 2

### Example of Personal Creedal Statement as model for student work (of shorter length)

Initially this was used as an introduction and reflection to start this unit for Year 9 Students. The students are invited to listen to this and to hold onto any images or phrases that resonate with them. They are asked to mentally identify statements that are spiritual or religious and those that are more personal and worldly. Thus the transcendent and the temporal, the sacred and secular, are later interweaved in their own personal statements. Following is an example of such a Creedal Statement.

>I believe in laughter in the rain.
>
>I believe in the first soft footfall and the thud of jellybean legs flailing as a child learns to walk.
>
>I believe in open arms; the entreaties of encouragement that are the refrains of a lifetime; the open arms of acceptance and welcome and refuge.
>
>I believe God is, was and will be.
>
>I believe in families: of blended configurations, the strange and strong tie of blood, the family circle of humanity, all God's children with their quirks and sparks and fitfulness and infinite variety – and my family of six siblings, grown now, and vastly different, held together by the glue and grace and grit of the shared history of rambunctious childhood and the benignly neglectful parental permission to be just who we were always going to be.
>
>I believe in small ecstasies and everyday wonders; the ordinary and daily gift-wrapped with joy when dawn breaks in violet and gold

sabres of light and birds chortle their canticles of gladness.

I believe in acts of faith, big and small.

I believe in the bunch of flowers picked with love from the garden; brave suburban jonquils, soft blushing pink camellias, big bossy gossipy hydrangeas, modest forget-me-nots.

I believe in God, the artist, and the infinite palette of Creation.

I believe in prayer; small beseechings, giant gratitude, the susurration, gentle as the flutter of angels' wings, of hope-filled breathings towards God.

I believe in old things: my mother's bald, glassy-eyed teddy who holds the secrets of her childhood and mine and my daughter's; books, dog-eared and tea-stained with strange illegible inscriptions as prizes for attendance at long ago Sunday schools; my grandmother's escritoire which holds and hides the memories of lives past; the me, who is not so far away, a mere half-century, from the freshly-laundered girl in the black and white Communion photo, beaming and buck-toothed and lit with hope.

I believe in new ideas – and old ideas, refreshed in the fluency of the zeitgeist, ready for another iteration, a new awakening.

I believe in favourite things; sad movies, puns, crumpets drowning in honey, the homeward-bound clatter of the train on a Saturday night, Elvis in black leather, the nourishing broth of good words, my daughter's hobgoblin laugh, middle-aged rock'n'rollers, rainbows.

I believe in children who share their lunches on the asphalt at lunchtime with the kids who don't have much.

I believe in blessings, bliss and Beatitudes.

I believe that God is on my side.

I believe in calloused and careworn hands, their years of work pressed into whorls of destiny and duty; hands, like my father's, that gently delivered babes into the arms of new mothers; the hands of my sister who can bring a canvas to life with a few deft stokes; helping hands and healing hands and the hands-up of my eager Year 9 students; my mother's hands that nursed and stroked and applauded; my husband's firm clasp; hands softly kneading rosary beads; the hands of salon and scullery, of making and doing, of clenching and holding and grabbing – and reaching beyond their grasp.

I believe in revelation, redemption and Resurrection.

I believe in quiet strength and gentle resistance and the occasional surge of outspoken audacity that breaks open closed minds.

I believe in the Catholic Church; sinning, shamed, chastened, diminished – unavoidably flawed and human.

I believe in forgiveness.

I believe in the Spirit – holy, encompassing, energising, lifting us to be better than we are.

I believe in good news and The Good News.

## Resources

*America Magazine* https://www.americamagazine.org/
Australian Catholic Bishops Conference https://www.catholic.org.au/
Archbishops' Office for Evangelisation https://www.cam1.org.au/evangelisation
*Australian Catholics* Magazine https://www.australiancatholics.com.au
CathNews https://cathnews.com/
Catholic Education 200 Years website https://200years.catholic.edu.au/
*Eureka Street* https://www.eurekastreet.com.au/
Garratt Publishing https://www.garrattpublishing.com.au/
Jesuit Media Australia https://www.jesuitmedia.org.au/
*Madonna* https://www.madonnamagazine.com.au/
Melbourne Archdiocese Catholic Schools https://www.macs.vic.edu.au/
National Centre for Evangelisation https://nce.catholic.org.au/
National Catholic Education Commission https://www.ncec.catholic.edu.au/
REsource MACS https://resource-macs.com/
*The National Catholic Reporter* (USA) https://www.ncronline.org/

*The Tablet* https://www.thetablet.co.uk/
*To Know Worship and Love* https://www.kwl.com.au/
*Understanding Faith* https://understandingfaith.edu.au/

# Glossary

| Word | Definition |
|---|---|
| *Ancien Règime* | The system of government before the French Revolution in 1789 where the nobility and Church paid few taxes and enjoyed a privileged and powerful status in French society. |
| Catechism | A catechism is a summary or exposition of doctrine and serves as a learning introduction to the Sacraments. It is traditionally used in catechesis, or Christian religious teaching of children and adult converts. |
| Charism | The spiritual personality of the religious community forged by and in its particular history. It identifies and animates this distinctive spirit, its special signature and its unique way of living out its mission in the world. |
| Discernment | The process of reflecting on the ordinary events in one's life in a prayerful manner, quietly attentive to the presence and action of God. The process is especially helpful in arriving at decision-making. |

| Word | Definition |
|---|---|
| Exegesis | Critical analysis and interpretation of a text, particularly scripture. This often uses an historical/social/contextual lens looking at theological implications and imperatives, language, purpose, audience, and sources. |
| Evangelist | Matthew, Mark, Luke, and John as the original evangelists who wrote the gospel narratives; one who aims to convert someone to the Christian faith, especially by preaching/ teaching. |
| Guardian Angel | A Guardian Angel is a type of angel that is considered as an angel assigned to protect and guide a particular person, group or nation. |
| Hermeneutics | Is the branch of theology that deals with the principles of biblical exegesis. |
| Limbo | Limbo is an intermediate abode between Heaven and Hell for the unbaptised outside of the presence of God, but free of the torment associated with Hell. More recently, the Church has dispensed with this concept. |
| Martyrdom | A person who chooses to suffer, even to die, rather than renounce his or her faith or Christian principles. |
| Monstrance | A vessel in which the consecrated eucharistic host (the sacramental bread) is carried in processions and is displayed during certain devotional ceremonies. |

Glossary

| Word | Definition |
|---|---|
| Morning Offering | A short prayer said at the start of each day to invoke the protection and help of God. |
| Rosary/rosary beads | The Rosary refers to a set of prayers used primarily in the Catholic Church, and to the physical string of knots or beads used to count the component prayers which consist of The Lord's Prayer and ten recitations of The Hail Mary in a set of five decades. |
| Sacraments | The Sacraments are chosen instruments of divine power and seen as outwards signs of inward grace as instituted by Jesus Christ. There are seven sacraments: Baptism, Confirmation, Holy Communion (Eucharist), Reconciliation (Confession), Anointing of the Sick, Holy Orders and Marriage. |
| Sanctuary | The sanctuary is the area around the altar in a church. |
| Scapular | Small sacramental scapulars of cloth that are worn daily under or over regular clothing as an open sign of devotion. They are generally blessed before being worn. |
| Sin | *Venial* sins wound our relationship with God. They are less serious than *mortal* sins which gravely impact this relationship and are seen as a repudiation of God's love. |

| Word | Definition |
|---|---|
| Tabernacle | The tabernacle is the place of the church that holds the *ciborium* (cup) containing the Eucharist. This makes the tabernacle the heart and the cornerstone of each church. |
| Transubstantiation | The complete change of the substance of bread and wine into the substance of Christ's body and blood by a validly ordained priest during the consecration at Mass. |
| Trinity | The Christian belief in the three persons of the Father, Son and Holy Spirit in which God exists. The persons of the Trinity are considered to be co-equal, co-existent and co-eternal. |
| Votive candles | Votive candles are small, short candles that are lit in church with the intention of praying for a person or cause. |
| Vatican II | The Second Vatican Council, also called Vatican II (1962–65), is the 21st Ecumenical Council of the Roman Catholic Church. It was announced by Pope John XXIII on 25 January 1959, as a means of spiritual renewal of the Church. |

www.ingramcontent.com/pod-product-compliance
Lightning Source LLC
Chambersburg PA
CBHW052055110526
44591CB00013B/2214